QUILTING FOR SHOW

KAREN McTAVISH

On~Word Bound Books
innovative publishing

DULUTH, MINNESOTA

QUILTING FOR SHOW Copyright © 2007 by Karen McTavish

The information in this book is presented in good faith, but the challenge of photographing quilts is monumental. The publishers of this book encourage the reader to view the quilts in person, if at all possible, as their portrayal here is limited by size and technology.

Photo credits:
On-Word Bound Books: Location photography, how-to images and quilt images unless otherwise mentioned. Inspirational and location photography taken in Duluth, MN.

Quilt images provided by Karen McTavish, Sharon Schamber, Ricky Tims, Linda Taylor, Hollis Chatelain, Caryl Bryer Fallert.

Diane Gaudynski quilt images reprinted with permission from American Quilters Society. *Through a Glass Darkly* by Diane Gaudynski, from *Guide to Machine Quilting,* American Quilters Society, 2002. Photo by Charles R. Lynch. *A Visit to Provence* by Diane Gaudynski, First Place Winner Miniature Quilt Category at the American Quilter's Society Quilt Show and Contest 2004. Photo by Charles R. Lynch, courtesy of the American Quilter's Society.

Alyssa Olson / Duluth, MN / alyssa.olson@gmail.com: Author bio photo.

Quilt spread border designs:
Patterns from *The Secrets of Elemental Quilting* by Karen McTavish
Published by On-Word Bound Books

Published by On-Word Bound Books / 803 E. 5th Street / Duluth, Minnesota 55805
www.onwordboundbooks.com

Library of Congress Cataloging-in-Publication Data

McTavish, Karen C.
  Quilting for show: a practical guide to successful competition quilting/ by Karen McTavish
    p. cm.
  ISBN 978-0-9744706-3-4 (pbk. : alk. paper) 1. Quilting--Patterns. 2. Patchwork--Patterns. 3. Appliqué--Patterns. 4. Patchwork quilts--Competitions. I. Title.
  TT835.M475 2007
  746.46'041--dc22
                          20061003191

Printed in the United States of America

DVD replicated in the United States of America

10 9 8 7 6 5 4 3 2 1

ACKNOWLEDGEMENTS

Many people have contributed their time and talents to this project
and to each, I thank you!

I would like to thank the dynamic duo - my editor, Sara Duke and my
publisher, David Devere of On-Word Bound Books for their help and
support with my books, their beautiful photography
and their dedication to this project.

And with great appreciation, a special thank you to Helen Squire for
writing the foreword with the panel of leaders in the quilting show world.
And thank you to Pepper Cory, Linda McCuean and Jean Carlton for
your informative contributions to this book.

I also want to thank my friends and family: the McTavish's, the Tash's,
the Krause's and the Quilters of Northern Minnesota.

A special thanks to AQPS for their continued support and for
manufacturing the best longarm quilting machine on the market.

For all the quilts we make, there is nothing more comforting
than to watch our children sleep under them.
~ Karen C. McTavish

TABLE OF CONTENTS

FOREWORD

BY HELEN SQUIRE

My involvement with quilting began in 1973 when I named my company Quilt-In®. You remember? When Love-In, Laugh-In and Sit-Ins were all the rage? The name sounded so original then, the play-on-words used to express the sense of communal happenings that old-fashioned quilting bees represented. My business motto was Quilt-In® for Fun & Fund Raising.

During the bicentennial, I already had an established quilt shop in Woodcliff Lake, New Jersey, and quilting was being listed under Colonial Crafts. I took my first class in judging quilts at an early quilt show held in Elmira, New York. Can you imagine? Bonnie Leman and Michael James were also in the class!

While leading a bus tour to the 1978 convention at Continental Quilt Congress in Washington DC, I attended the first public showing of machine piecing. It was a magnificent star design that was hung unquilted, stretched around a wooden frame so that the back as well as the front could be viewed and admired! This was at a time when there were no categories at quilt shows for anything sewn by machine.

Acceptance did not come easily for machine quilting. It took more than ten years until Caryl Bryer Fallert machine pieced and machine quilted CORONA II: SOLAR ECLIPSE and entered it in the 5th AQS Annual Quilt Show & Contest in Paducah, Kentucky. It won Best of Show and traditional quilters were aghast!

Seventeen years later, when SEDONA ROSE by Sharon Schamber—a longarm quilter—won, there was hardly a peep. Sharon is the first quilter to win two major prizes in the same AQS Quilt Show & Contest. In 2006, SEDONA ROSE won the Best of Show award and SCARLET SERENADE was the Longarm Machine Quilting prizewinner.

Why is this? What happened? I asked friends in the quilting industry whom I admire, and whose opinions I value, to comment **on the most exciting change(s) in judging at quilt shows as it applies to machine quilting.** A panel of twelve experts shared their views on what's happening—the difference twenty plus years have made in judging the prizewinning, show-stopping quilts being made by quilters on domestic, midarm, and longarm quilting machines today.

"Machine quilting has finally come into its own," according to **Gerald E. Roy**, quilt judge, author and AQS certified appraiser. "It has been around long enough to be perfected into an art form. The best machine quilting is now comparable to the best hand quilting."

Helen Smith Stone, show producer and owner of Quilting on the Waterfront ~ Machines in Motion, Duluth, Minnesota, feels that "machine quilting is now accepted as an artistic, creative, and appropriate way to 'quilt the quilt.'"

"I suppose the most exciting change of all is that machine quilted quilts are now held by most knowledgeable quilters in much the same regard as hand quilted ones," states **Diane Gaudynski**, the winner of numerous first prizes and best of shows, author of two best-selling books, and a featured quilter in this very book. She is the only four-time winner of the prestigious Machine Workmanship Award at the AQS show.

> Years ago they were relegated to categories that were either all machine quilted and considered second rate at best, or even lumped in with tied quilts. The artistry and degree of difficulty in pulling off a well-done machine-quilted quilt is now respected. This came about because we machine quilters rose to the standards expected of the best hand-quilted quilts. We did not accept the premise that machine quilting is inferior and shoddy, something that is a make-do measure or simply a fast and fun way to finish a top. We put our hearts and souls into making it as beautiful as possible, something that will stand the test of time, and be an art in its own right, sharing the stage with hand-quilted masterpieces. Twenty years ago I was reluctant to admit I was a machine quilter, and now it is something I embrace with pride.

Bonnie K. Browning, AQS executive show director, author, and judge, noticed on the entry forms for the 22nd Annual AQS Quilt Show and Contest that an overwhelming 72% of the quilts juried into the competition were made by machine. "The break down was 56% on domestic home machines, 16% on longarm, and 28% by hand."

An overdue new trend in quilt show categories is the listing of both the quiltmaker and the quilter. "Recognition! The most exciting change for me has been that standup machine quilters are finally receiving the recognition they deserve," notes **Marcia Stevens**, founder of the Machine Quilters Showcase and *Unlimited Possibilities* magazine. "Too many shows did not specifically acknowledge the quilter if it happened to be someone other than the quiltmaker. The quality of machine quilting has improved dramatically and viewers are finally embracing it."

"The most important change is that the machine quilter is being recognized as part of the award process," echoes **Ann Collet**, The Home Machine Quilting Show (HMQS) owner/director, Centerville, Utah.

> If the quilt is pieced and owned by one person and quilted by another person, recognition in the form of ribbons and prize money needs to be given to both as each contributes to the finished quilt. After all 'Quilting does make the quilt.' Lately that dual recognition is becoming more of the standard.

The panel was also asked **what qualifications or credentials do you look for in quilt judges today?** "Experience" was the overwhelming answer! "Nothing replaces having viewed and evaluated quilts in many shows," said Bonnie Browning. Some wanted them to have experience as a machine quilter as well as be an experienced judge. Some looked for judging certification or at least knowledge of all aspects of the quilt field and expertise in her (his) specialties. Credentials were requested, and a list of the shows they had judged previously.

Other comments were:

> Because I am involved and promote standup machine quilting, I look for judges who either own a quilting machine or are very familiar with the capabilities and intricacies of standup quilting so they can fairly judge all machine-quilting categories. —Marcia Stevens

> I regard experience as a quilter, recognition for their work either by awards won in judged competitions or by esteem they have earned by their peers in the quilting industry. An all-around grounded knowledge of quilt history as well as art and design principles is also really important, as is expertise in the technical points of quilt making and fair-mindedness for all styles of quilts and the opinions of the other judges. —Diane Gaudynski

> Personally, I look at the judge's own ability to enter and win in quilt shows. There is more credibility if the judge has been on the other end of the judging process. I think the best judges are award-winning quilters. I also think today's judges should be up with the times, judging in the 21st century and aware of the trends today, since these are times that we live in now. —**Linda V. Taylor**, producer/host of *Linda's Longarm Quilting*, award-winning quilter, author, and master longarm quilting teacher

In the judging questionnaire, I asked if they had **any advice to share from a judge's point of view**. Their wisdom is expressed in the following excerpts:

> Organization of the judging process by the facilitator is essential, especially if it is a large competition, including: enough helpers to assist in an efficient way with the handling of the quilts; good scribes to record notes; a physical setup with good lighting, low stress flooring, enough equipment, such as tables, etc.; making the process as comfortable and expeditious as possible; sufficient time allotment for the judging without over-exerting the judges; water and other amenities that keep everyone going and happy. Since judging is such a key factor in the outcome of a quilt show or competition, I feel the treatment and pampering of the judges is not only important but also essential. —Ann Collet

> On the quilt entry form, show organizers should try to find out as much as possible about the machine used in the quilting of the quilt—specifically, is it a sit-down or standup quilting machine, fully computerized machine, or hand guided. I believe that information should be passed on to the judges. I have also always felt that the judges should have the description of the quilt read to them if it sheds light on the construction or techniques used, giving the judges more insight on the quilt. —Marcia Stevens

> The perfect judge has to have the ability to put personal preferences and prejudices aside during the judging process; recognize extraordinary work even if it does not reflect current trends; weigh technical skills and visual skills equally; have the vocabulary and the ability to use it in order to convey their criticism or praise to a quiltmaker using objective terms (no like or dislike—not appropriate); and be confident enough to stand up to opposition if the occasion requires it. —Gerald Roy

If you make something that is your passion, research it to get your techniques mastered and correct, and pay attention to details like square corners and straight seams, chances are it will do much better in judging than if you try to figure out a formula for 'what will win.' Stay true to what you love, whether it is style, color, or design, and your piece will rise to a new level because you are working on something that you care about. Follow your instincts; don't try to please your friends in your Bee! Stay focused; work on one thing and do it well. —Diane Gaudynski

Don't make a quilt with the judges in mind. Judges try very hard to not let their personal preferences enter into the judging process. Don't take the critique as cast in stone. Remember it is only the judge's opinion, not the law. Do make quilts to please yourself, the ultimate judge. —**Libby Lehman**, judge, *Threadplay* author, and award-winning quilter

Judging a quilt show is one of the hardest things I have ever done, probably because I compete so much and I know how it feels to be in the hot seat. It upsets me when people complain about the judges or bemoan the fact that they didn't win. Judging a quilt show is always subjective. A quilt could win or lose in any quilt show depending on the judge's own preferences. Of course, it's always exciting to win; but if you can't be a good loser and congratulate the winner, you shouldn't enter. I believe judges do the best they can and try very hard to always be fair. —Linda Taylor

As a judge, take the job seriously, as quilters will value your opinion. Be kind, yet provide constructive feedback. Take your time—be thorough. —Helen Smith Stone

Now let's talk about what you, the quilter, need to think about when you enter a competition or show. When asked to **rate the importance of eight areas of concern**, the unanimous feeling was that good workmanship outscored good design. A well-made quilt—a potential prizewinner—should have:

> Balanced quilting areas: no hills, valleys or large unquilted areas
> No rippling: hangs or lies flat with squared corners
> A chosen quilting design that enhances the top
> Even-sized stitching with controlled starts and stops
> Enough structural quilting for the size of the project
> No marks showing: guidelines, tracings and/or pounce powder have been removed
> Original or unique quilting design(s)
> Thread use appropriate to the fabric, theme, or artistic interpretation of the piece

Additional areas to consider are: Was the quilting done with a computerized machine or hand guided? Are the special techniques well executed? Was the thread tension as optimal as possible—with little or no "unbalanced" stitches and without color showing from the opposite side?

There are always two points of view on any subject. Some look for visual skills, i.e., color, balanced asymmetrical designs, composition, etc., while others look for perfect piecing, beautiful appliqué, and/or creativity and originality of the quilting design.

"Good workmanship is most important in all aspects of the quilt…," states **Holice Turnbow,** who was one of the first quilt teachers and designers to be certified as a quilt judge by the National Quilting Association. He continues, "…no matter how extraordinary the machine quilting is, it becomes ordinary if the quality of the base (top) is poor."

However, Gerald Roy, co-founder of the Pilgrim/Roy Collection, believes that a quilt can be successful even if the borders wobble slightly or the batting does not extend fully to the edges of the binding.

It is the quilt show founders and their professional organizations that enable us to shine and grow as quilters. It's mind-boggling to realize that Quilts, Inc., the American Quilter's Society, and Mancuso Show Management during this time have accrued a combined total of 70 years and over 200 shows, providing a showcase for quilts and their prizewinners. There is even a quilt museum. The Museum of the American Quilter's Society in Paducah, Kentucky, was established in 1991 to feature prizewinning quilts from AQS shows in ever-changing exhibits.

The quality of the machine quilting has improved in both the control and amount of quilting on each quilt. It is amazing to see such beautiful allover stitching. But we are looking for the best quilt, which includes design, color, and quilting. We have the same high standards for the best workmanship awards. We look at all the elements, whether it is quilted by hand or machine quilted. —**Meredith Schroeder**, founder and president of the American Quilter's Society; AQS Quilt Show & Contest, Paducah, Kentucky, and Quilt Expo, Nashville, Tennessee

The rapid growth of machine quilting has resulted in a side effect none of us expected, and that is a complete change of perspective in the way we view quilts at shows. We are now so accustomed to seeing the incredible amount and complexity of machine quilting on a quilt that our eye demands similar quilting on fine hand-quilted quilts, even when this is not really appropriate. Intellectually, we know that the hand-quilted quilt does NOT need more quilting, but visually, the eye requires it. It's a true anomaly.

When we introduced the Husqvarna Viking Gallery of Quilt Art at the International Quilt Festival in Houston in 2002, it was the first time machine-quilted quilts had been given a prestigious showcase all their own, and that gallery, which has resulted in these beautiful quilts being toured all over the U.S. and Europe, can take credit for introducing many people to artistic machine quilting rather than the utilitarian machine quilting of the past. —**Karey Bresenhan**, director of International Quilt Festival–Houston and Chicago and International Quilt Markets; co-director of Patchwork & Quilt Expo–Europe

We have been astonished as to the size of the (quilt) market and the growth of our company. Machine quilting has certainly become a prominent element in the competition arena. However, what is most impressive in the quilting world is the passion of the quilt artists who are creating the entries displayed at our competitions. —**David and Peter Mancuso**, Mancuso Show Management, New Hope, Pennsylvania; promoters of

Pennsylvania National Quilt Extravaganza, Pacific International Quilt Festival, Mid-Atlantic Quilt Festival, and other regional shows

Quilting is a passionate subject. All the areas we have mentioned are equally important and will of necessity vary with each individual quilt. The WOW factor of a quilt—the instant realization that the sum really is greater than the total of all parts—must prevail.

I encourage everyone to enter quilt shows and eagerly await the judges' critiques. It is your chance to learn to improve your work, as you read their comments. Honestly look at the winning quilts. Realize what yours might have lacked. With experience gained, you too may be the next award winner!

Known as the "Dear Helen, Can You Tell Me...?" columnist, I have answered questions for many years. I have authored eight books of quilting designs with over 750 published patterns. It is a great pleasure when I see a show quilt quilted with one of my designs. I have also enjoyed the challenge of editing the AQS Golden Threads Series of quilting books for a talented group of longarm machine quilters: Janie Donaldson, Cheryl Barnes, Sally Terry, Judy Allen, Keryn Emmerson, Sue Patten and Pam Clarke.

I know quilting and I know quilters, and this I can tell you: **Karen McTavish** is a unique personality who, in a very short time, has made a lasting contribution to quiltmaking. It is indeed an honor to be asked to write the foreword for her newest book, *Quilting for Show*.

KAREN'S STORY

*T*he mailman is leaving my driveway. He brought me a box. On this warm, sunny, spring afternoon I go to my knees outside my studio. Inside the box, a quilt appears with a big burgundy ribbon attached to it. It says, "Teacher's Choice." The year is 1999—only 2 years after I started quilting. It was the first time I entered a quilt in a show. I went nuts. My daughter, who thought I had set myself on fire, came running out of the house to find her mother jumping up and down in the yard, screaming her head off, holding a ribbon in her hand while collapsing in tears. This was my experience with winning my first ribbon. I acted like a crazy person and was bathed in joy.

I have asked many quilters to describe their experience with winning a ribbon. When I asked them if they remember what they were doing when they found out that their quilt won an award, they all said, "Yes, of course I remember exactly what I was doing!" But when I asked other questions, such as "How did it affect you as a quilter? How does ribboning make you feel about yourself?" The answer to these questions is generally the same: "There is nothing else I can compare it to" or "I have no idea how to answer that question." I think the reason why it's hard to explain what it really "feels" like to win a quilting ribbon, is that in the backs of our minds, we think somebody screwed up somewhere and there has been a terrible mistake.

We just can't wrap our brains around the idea that we are good enough to be an award winning quilter. After the insecurities and apprehension disappear and our heads quiet down a little, we can be practical about what is ahead. A new identity forms as you realize that you are officially an award winning quilter. What a title! Do you have the emotional stability to add that to your list of accomplishments? Sure, you do.

Once, while walking through a quilt show, I heard a woman say, "I think it is so brave for anyone to enter a quilt in a quilt show, for all to see and for all to judge. How fearless!" She's right. Entering a quilt in a show can be very tough emotionally. We *are* brave quilters to have "the entire world" see our flaws and imperfections. However, critiques are not meant to be painful but helpful. I don't feel ripped apart or insecure by examining eyes. I don't even feel ripped apart by judges' comments. The true reason to enter shows is to get a critique of your work. The critique will tell you what you really need to hear and what you need to work on. The next step is to go take a class or buy a book on the subject where the critique claims, "Needs improvement."

I have a wall in my studio where I display my quilting ribbons. I have won Best of Show, 1st Place, 2nd Place, 3rd Place, Sweepstakes, Viewer's Choice, Best Machine Quilting, Teacher's Awards and Honorable Mentions from state to international levels but the most important ribbon on my wall is my very first ribbon—my "Teacher's Choice." It was given to me by someone I had never heard of at the time. I didn't know who the teacher was because I just felt so drunk with power after receiving it, that I couldn't make the connection. A few years ago, I was re-hanging my ribbons and realized that my "Teacher's Choice" was from Linda Taylor. She has no idea how that ribbon changed my world. It turned a self-doubting, insecure quilter into a confident artist. As a result of that ribbon, I was able to really focus on my quilting career. That burgundy ribbon gave me the confidence to move on with my life. As a single mother, as a self-employed quilter and as a person, it gave me the reassurance that I'd be okay. Who would have known that such a little ribbon could do all that?

It's a strange world you enter when you compete with other quilts. Your quilt becomes the "work" or the "piece," not a blanket your kid sleeps under. You are no longer the hobby quilter, but an artist. Painters are not judged on the excellent construction of their tightly pulled canvas. Artists are not judged on the number of brush strokes used in a painting or the number of staples used to hold together the canvas. But quilters are judged equally on good construction and knowledge of their craft as well as artistic originality and skill.

This book was written as a guide for any quilter looking for information about what is involved in quilting for show: what are some things you'll need to know about entering your quilts in shows, what it takes to be an award winning quilter, and what an award winning quilt looks like. The quilts displayed in this book are from first-timers to master quilters. This book offers suggestions based on my experience with shows, judges and the quilting industry. These suggestions should help you feel informed and confident in your journey of entering your quilts in show. Sometimes you have to do the hardest thing to achieve the greatest success in life. So squeeze your eyes shut, and just do it. Best of Show wishes!

SPRINGTIME IN CLOVER VALLEY (84" x 84")

AWARDS:

Innovations: 1st Place, Teachers Exhibit Professional, 2002

*C*lover Valley, on the north shore of Lake Superior, is the township where my family resides. The "square in a square" inspiration came from a mother/daughter trip to the International Quilt show in Houston. The idea came together on the flight home to Minnesota. My mother loves color, unlike her daughter who prefers white. I wanted to quilt a wholecloth using shadow trapunto, but had construction problems from the start. The options for a large, shadow-trapunto, wholecloth quilt are very limited because there are not large width fabrics available in batiste. My mother had to piece the simple "square in a square" using 60 inch wide, Swiss batiste fabric. This quilt uses shadow trapunto to create the different colors; it does not have dyed batting. The batiste cotton quilt top was originally all white but when neon fabrics are inserted between the quilting layers, color appears. Once the quilting is complete, the color really comes to the forefront. My mother used miniature piecing in the sashing, which strategically hid the white seams of the batiste and the raw edges of the neon fabrics. This quilt won my mother's first blue ribbon in a national competition.

~ Karen McTavish with Janet McTavish

GETTING STARTED

As a longarm machine quilter, who has run a machine quilting business for over 10 years, I receive quilts from other quilters who piece the top, and I design (the quilting motifs) and quilt the quilt. When I receive a quilt top that has incredible beauty, excellent construction and takes my breath away, I always bring up the option of putting the quilt in show to the owner of the quilt. Here are some details I look for when considering if a quilt is eligible for competition:

Does the quilt hang straight?

Are the appliqué stitches invisible?

Is the piecing precise
and well constructed?

Does the quilt have a good first impression or strong visual impact?

Is this an original design or a commercial quilt kit purchased at a quilt shop?

These are the things I think about before I design the quilting for the quilt. Let's face it, if I know that the quilt I am working on will be judged on a national level, it's got to be my very best work. This quilt may take 2-4 weeks for me to design, quilt and finish. Historically, 2-4 weeks is nothing compared to the hundreds of hours that it would take for a hand quilter. There is no way to be an award winning quilter and take short cuts. If I am giving a quilt to a baby, I would design the quilt for a baby so the quilt will last. If I am

quilting a quilt for a customer knowing it will go to a quilt show, I will quilt for the judge. If I do my best work and do the hardest thing, I am usually rewarded. Or at the very least, I have created a one of a kind heirloom quilt.

COLLECTING IDEAS FOR INSPIRATION

I go to great lengths to find motivation. I try to not copy from other quilts and to stay as original as possible to keep the judges' attention. Here are some ideas of where you can gain inspiration and find designs to incorporate into a quilt:

Art Nouveau designs (Dover books, copy right free designs)

Aging library books featuring older, traditional quilts

Architectural elements

Stone and wood scrollwork

Fence and iron work

Ceiling tiles

Elaborate rugs

Churches

Victorian homes

Museums

Tombstones

Pin striping

Tattoos – tribal to floral

Appliqué floral designs converted into quilting designs

Stencils of any kind – quilting, room décor, decorative or self drawn

BLUE MEN (78" x 58")

AWARDS: IQA: Master Award for Contemporary Artistry, 2001
QTQ: 1st Place Wholecloth, 2002
AQS: Brother International Machine Workmanship Award, 2003

While living in Burkina Faso, Mali and Benin, I befriended many Tuareg men who are traditionally nomads who roam the Sahara Desert carrying goods from North Africa to Sub-Saharan Africa. They make beautiful handcrafts from leather and steel. We spent so many hours together laughing and drinking Tuareg tea! The nickname "blue men" has been given to these proud men because they typically wear indigo blue turbans to protect themselves from the sun and the sand storms when they cross the desert on their camels. The indigo in the fabric rubs off on their skin and sometimes gives them a blue tint. This quilt is a tribute to my Tuareg friends. This is a wholecloth quilt, painted only with blue dye. The many colors of thread in the quilting give it a touch of reality. ~ *Hollis Chatelain*

Blue Men is a pictorial, painted, wholecloth wall hanging. While it is a stunning quilt, finding a show category for a quilt like this could be a challenge. Some shows don't have a wholecloth category for painted quilts while other shows would allow it. Generally, wholecloth is considered to be one element—quilting without embellishments. *Blue Men* could be entered as a pictorial wall hanging; however, its dimensions are slightly larger than most shows' wall hanging size limits. Many shows have a hand quilting category this quilt would qualify for, but this quilt is machine quilted and often there is not a category for just machine quilting. You may find that the only category in which to enter a complicated quilt like this is First Time Entrant. This way your quilt will follow the show's guidelines and not be rejected for not fitting in a category! In this case, being innovative did not deter the shows from accepting the quilt, or the judges from awarding it.

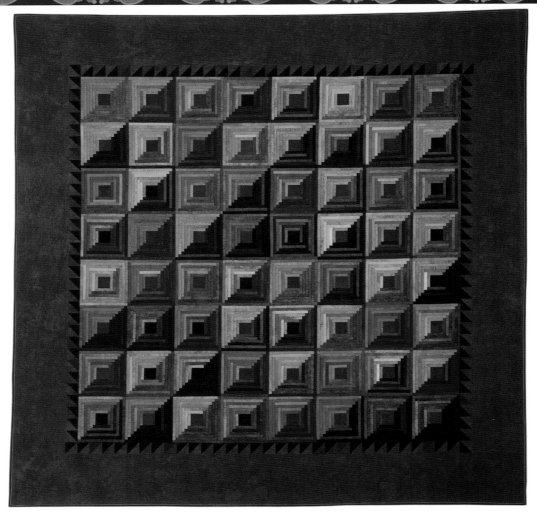

Through a Glass, Darkly: An American Memory (81" x 81")

$\mathcal{M}$ade in 2001 with hand-dyed Cherrywood® fabrics, this log cabin quilt evokes memories of our American heritage. The original border feather designs spring from a Victorian pitcher with an English staghound as the handle, with Welsh spiral motifs symbolizing life's eternal cycles.

The central portion was quilted "in the ditch" free-motion so the quilting lines wouldn't detract from the color play created by the colors and their placement in the blocks. The straight lines quilted in the block centers reflect the geometry of the blocks.

The border design was quilted with several shades of #100 silk thread to add depth and luster to the hand dyed cotton. The curves and flow of the feathers contrast softly with the stark geometry of the interior. When viewed at a distance, the quilt is reminiscent of light passing through a dark stained glass window with bits of lighter colors distributed over the surface like fractured sunlight. The log cabin pattern is an intrinsic part of American quilt history and this version celebrates its graphic simplicity and elegance. The log cabin has a certain "humbleness" that is very appealing yet provides a tried and true sense of sophisticated design.

I tried to make this a quilt that celebrates the foundations of our quilting heritage in America. The light shining through is our American spirit, the spirit of those pioneer women Quiltmakers who came before us, and the spirit of the country today that will take us forward through the times to come.

Judges' Comments: Fabulous fabrics, stunning; Exquisite visual impact, outstanding color choice and placement, pieced with precision, quilting design in center of blocks and borders unusual and beautifully done; Beautifully, beautifully, totally wonderful in every sense; Impeccable quilting, piecing and color scheme; Marvelous quilting, wonderful skills, love the colors; should be seen in a gallery setting to fully appreciate.

My feelings: "I think this quilt touches people. It is warm and deep, not only in color, but in mood and sense. The tactile suede-like fabrics invite you to stroke it, and the warm subtle aura it projects makes you want to keep on returning for another gaze. It's not busy and overdone. It doesn't try too hard. It is a real quilt, a quilt that can go on a bed and be loved and slept under, yet the art of it makes it something to cherish and display and look at and appreciate as art. Because it is the simplest pieced design, many can relate to it and understand how it works, yet still be intrigued by its complexity. It sums up my feelings about 'what is a quilt' perfectly." ~*Diane Gaudynski*

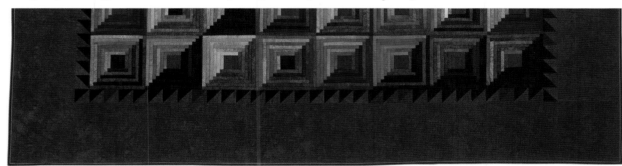

AWARDS: QOTW: First Place, 2001
QOTW: Ricky Tims Faculty Ribbon, 2001
IQA: Pfaff Master Award for Machine Artistry, 2001
Thirty Quilt Artists of the World Exhibit: Tokyo, Japan, 2002
AQS: First Place Traditional Pieced, 2002
NQA: Masterpiece Quilt, 2002
NQA: First Place and Best of Show, 2002
Lowell Quilt Festival: Jean Ray Laury Faculty Ribbon "Images," 2004

*T*his quilt will blow your mind. I was actually standing in front of Diane's quilt at Quilting on the Waterfront in 2001 when Ricky Tims placed his Teacher's Ribbon on the quilt before the show opened. It was like watching history in the making. Diane has influenced quilters around the world and has changed the face of quilting today with her feather artistry. Beyond her mastery of the craft, Diane has a fun tradition of quilting her "signature." Not her actual signature, but possibly her initials or a curled up cat, or both. Whenever I see one of her quilts my first mission is to find where she hid her "signature." It's a quilter's version of an inside joke. If you find the cat, you know Diane a little bit better than you did before.

BOHEMIAN RHAPSODY (86" x 86")

Bohemian Rhapsody began as a small original paper-cut style medallion block. A border was added to create a small wall quilt. Improvising on the theme, the quilt continued to grow. The undulating symmetry is loosely based on a traditional Diamond in a Square. The urns and other appliquéd motifs create large circular effects. *Bohemian Rhapsody* is made from original, 100% cotton, hand-dyed fabrics. It is machine pieced, machine appliquéd and machine quilted with silk and rayon threads. Ironically, the original medallion from which the quilt emerged was replaced. ~ *Ricky Tims*

AWARDS: International Quilt Festival: 1st Prize Innovative Appliqué-Large, 2002
Mid-Atlantic Quilt Festival: Best use of Color-Innovative Quilt, 2003
AQS: 1st Prize Appliqué-Professional, 2003
Rockome Gardens: Best of Show, 2003
Road to California: Judges' Merit, 2004
QOTW: Best of Show, 2004
AQS: Wall Calendar, 2004

When I first saw this quilt I was completely blown away. Ricky's fearless use of contrasting threads is second to none. When you see a quilt by Ricky Tims, you notice the excellent construction and the originality, which set his quilts apart. Ricky is also a leader in earning top awards for domestic machine quilting. View his website to see his fabric line, quilt gallery and to hear some of his music.

WHAT DOES THE QUILT SAY TO YOU

Something I like to keep in mind when I am designing a quilt for competition is tradition. For example, I don't want to quilt nudes unless I am entering the quilt in an art show. Generally, I try not to rock the boat too much and I try to stay on top of the quilting trends. There is no magic formula for figuring out what the current trends are in the quilt world. Keep your eyes peeled at quilt shows for the Best of Show quilts; these quilts are examples of what the judges are looking for. An observation I can make is that most Best of Show quilts have trapunto, appliqué or both incorporated into the quilt. Before I get started on a quilt top I ask myself some questions:

Is the quilt traditional or contemporary? And, does the quilting need to match the quilt top style?

Yes. If it's a very traditional quilt, the apple cannot fall too far from the tree. Respect tradition - the judges do.

Does the quilting design historically work with your quilt top?

Judges appreciate freehand over all patterns on a quilt top when appropriate, but for show quilts, a well planned and thought out quilting design will be more pleasing. Respecting tradition would challenge you to attain the "hand quilted look" even through you are using a machine. You may want to do some research on the origins of the quilt, how it was quilted when it first appeared in the quilting world, then make your 21st century flourishes and awesome additions to make it

your own. Respecting tradition could mean using matching threads, instead of a loud contrast. On the other hand, it's fashionable to use contrasting threads in innovative or contemporary quilts.

Should I use a busy print for a backing?

Yes, Yes, Yes. Using a busy print for your backing fabric will help you hide imperfections, stops and starts and tension issues in the quilting.

Will this quilt be enhanced by trapunto?

If the quilt top has plenty of plain space where the quilting designs can really be seen, then this could be a show stopping quilt. Trapunto, added under appliqué and quilting motifs, is such a magnificent addition to the quilt that the judges will be more than happy to honor you with a prize. When I haven't used trapunto my critiques have stated that the quilt "could be enhanced by trapunto."

Are you completely intimidated and panic stricken by your quilt top?

If the answer is yes, then this is a show quilt. By the end of the process, you will feel more confident in your quilting ability. There is always that little voice in the back of your head telling you that you cannot achieve this. Don't listen. Forge ahead anyway. When the binding is on, you will know you created something glorious and you have two years from the day of its last stitch to compete with it.

YELLOW AND WHITE IRISH CHAIN (111" x 112")

Susan Henderson is one of my favorite customers; her piecing work is always impeccable. When she brought this quilt to my studio and said, "Do whatever!" I was in Heaven. The wide border and open blocks left plenty of room for play, and her willingness to give me free rein allowed my imagination to soar. Since the Irish Chain is such a great blank palette for innovative design work and has such a strong graphic presence, I felt that this quilt could hold its own against a whole birdful of feathers, so I threaded my quilting machine, dropped the needle, and hit the gas. All of the quilting designs are completely freehand with very minimal marking in the borders. Each block is filled with feathers in differing configurations, and the border is filled with flowing, twirling, curling feathers. I did a simple continuous curve in the chains to add a sense of balance to all of the feather work. Overall, the effect is one of tremendous movement and grace, and is very pleasing to the eye of the viewer.

In its first competition, this quilt won Best Longarm Machine Quilting, and was given excellent scores in all categories by the panel of judges. Comments included, "Beautiful Feathers!" and "Well Pieced!" so I think that this quilt truly 'had it all' when it came to competition. It is such a blessing for me to have a customer who does a beautiful job on her end, and trusts me to do a good job on my end. ~ *Kim Brunner with Susan Henderson (piecer)*

AWARDS: Minnesota State Quilt Show: Best Longarm Machine Quilting Award, 2005
MQS: Teacher's Ribbon, 2005

In the longarm world, one of the greatest achievements you could ever hope for is being awarded with the Best of Show – Longarm Machine Quilting award in a national show. It is possibly the greatest feeling in the world. This award will shoot down all your insecurities as a quilter and make you walk on air for a good 10 days after. Maybe 11 days, probably 12. The most important ingredients needed to win this award are excellent tension, good stops and starts and original quilting designs that are fairly intense.

Do the hardest thing + never take a short cut = Best of Show – Longarm.

TUESDAY AFTERNOON (53" x 57")

When I created *Tuesday Afternoon* I used mainly batik fabrics. I layered the quilt with one layer of Hobbs 80/20 and then one layer of Quilter's Dream Poly. The quilt uses Superior Threads throughout. The bead work was done by hand, stitched in the wee hours when I couldn't sleep. This was when the name came as well. I had an "old" tune in my head. Any one remember it? Living in the southwest, the fabrics were a delight to my eyes, as was the pattern. The bright orange fabric was a perfect place to start the quilting design. The remainder of the designs came as I quilted one area and moved onto the next. Nothing was predetermined - the designs just happened. I really enjoy creating spaces in a quilt. It produces unexpected interest and draws the eye around the entire piece. This was also the first quilt that I had quilted for myself in (at the time) 6 years of longarm quilting for others. Some judges' comments were: Good Visual Impact; Piecing well done; Choice of quilting designs enrich the quilt; Beading adds interest; Well chosen color and placement.

- Myrna Ficken and Virginia Affleck

*T*his piece is beautiful in a couple of ways. The beadwork is delicate yet bright; it is not overwhelming but truly compliments the piecing. Another element is the geometric quilting designs which are perfect for a quilt that has curves and circles. This looks like a nicely planned out quilting design—which for Myrna was not planned at all but instinctive. Some quilters just have that creative flow and need no plan. As a result, we see the judges are happy with the overall impact the quilt made on them.

AWARDS: MQS: 2nd Place Wall, 2005
Las Vegas Guild Quilt Show: 2nd Place, 2005
Las Vegas Guild Quilt Show: Viewer's Choice Award, 2005
Road to California: 3rd Place Wall, 2006.

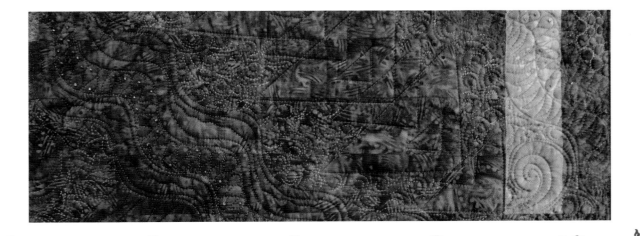

WHAT JUDGES WANT

Simply, the judges want you to blow their socks off.

Try to remember that you can't please everyone. Each judge has a personal preference and they all have different tastes when it comes to quilting. You will never know why one quilt ribboned but the other didn't. Sometimes it boils down to the judge and the judge's taste in quilts. There are so many different criteria for a quilt to win or not to win that it feels like guess work unless you have the critique in front of you. The greatest thing I discovered while researching the judging world is that not all judges agree on what makes a great quilt. Each judge has their own opinion and judging style. I know if a quilting judge likes my work they may be a judge who machine quilts. I may have a better chance at ribboning with this judge than if I was judged by a hand quilter. If I don't ribbon and can't figure out why, I'll throw my quilt in another show to see what will happen. I will usually ribbon at the next show. This happens all the time with show quilts. Sometimes they do well in some parts of the country, then in other shows they fizzle. That's the name of the game. Below is a gathering of critiques that I have collected throughout the years. This isn't a check list but it should give you an idea of what judges want to see. Remember, there is no "Quilt God," just lots of opinions on this subject. Take what you want, and leave the rest. Bear in mind, it gets a little picky from here.

OVER-ALL IMPACT/FIRST IMPRESSION/WORKMANSHIP

Appliqué stitches tight and appliqué is smooth appearing
Piecing/appliqué thread does not show
Grain of fabric accurately placed
Special techniques executed well
Excellent visual impact
Accurate piecing of borders
Embellishments/embroidery well done
Sashing and borders are even and straight
Quilt hangs straight and outside edges should be flat
Evidence that the quilt maker understands medium used
Quilt is clean without stains or markings and free of odors
Quilting fits spaces uniformly and complements the pieced design

DESIGN AND COLOR

Colors are balanced and appropriate for quilt
Fabric choices enhance quilt style
Design is original
Focal point of quilt is well planned
Embellishments should not detract from impact

THE PIECING

Quilt should have good construction in piecing
Points and triangles should have sharp points
Seam allowances pressed consistently and lay flat
Intersections meet perfectly
Good tension in piece work
Borders must be straight and blocks and cornerstones well aligned
Thread color used to sew the fabric together should blend with the fabrics

APPLIQUÉ

Appliqué elements should be well placed and align accurately
Curves are smooth and rounded nicely
Thread color matching with the appliqué
Appliqué markings are not visible

QUILTING DESIGN AND QUILTING STITCHES

Quilting is well thought out and complements the pieced design
Stops and starts should be undetectable and unobtrusive
Quilting design marks should not be visible
Appropriate quilting design and style
Consistent stitch length overall
Good tension of quilting
Good backtracking
Effective thread choice
Straight lines are straight and parallel lines parallel
*Many judges want to see knots (starts and stops) buried.

FINISHING/BINDINGS

Binding is filled with batting to the edge; binding should not have any ripples in fabric
Bindings should be ¼ inch wide finished, indistinguishable from the front and back
Binding corners should be square and even with front and back sewn closed
Miters on border should align with the miter on the binding
Hand stitches should be even and invisible
Corner miters should be sewn closed
Binding techniques are well mastered
Piping and binding embellishments are executed well
*Some judges like to see bias binding and will look for the bias in the grain.

Midnight Fantasy #6
(59" x 48")

AWARDS:
AQS 20th Anniversary show: Best Machine Workmanship Award (Wall Quilt), 2004

The design for this quilt came during a sleepless night when I got out of bed and made a series of ten small drawings to pass the time. One of those drawings was refined to create the design for this quilt. This is the sixth quilt in a series based on those midnight drawings. The final design was enlarged and drawn full size on a four by five foot rectangular piece of freezer paper to create the templates for this quilt. Much of this quilt was pieced directly onto

the long curving paper templates, following pencil lines drawn on the back to achieve precision. Before piecing, I cut strips of fabric in color and value (light to dark) gradations and laid them out on my ironing table in arrangements I call intersecting color and value gradations. The areas between this complex piecing were then filled with larger pieces of fabric which were hand painted with dye in many different patterns and colors. There are many areas where long sweeping curves seem transparent in places where they cross. This illusion was created by carefully selecting fabrics for those templates in colors that blended the colors of two curves that appear to cross. Fabrics in more than a hundred different colors and patterns were used. More than fifty different colors of polyester and acrylic top stitching thread were used for the quilting. This quilt was made as a special commission for the home of Suzie Phillips. ~ *Caryl Bryer Fallert*

Caryl is the one of the great quilt show pioneers of machine quilting. In 1989, Caryl's quilt, *Corona #2: Solar Eclipse* won Best of Show at AQS in Paducah. She was the first contemporary art quilter to win the Best of Show award at AQS, using a domestic sewing machine to quilt her quilt. Because AQS was considered a very traditional show 18 years ago, there was considerable controversy and backlash mainly because the quilt was machine quilted. The quilting world was shocked. Caryl recalls that about 1 out of every 6 quilters who approached her had something negative to say about the quilt. However, she also heard numerous whispered comments from the professional quilters of the world, that they could now go home and finish their quilts by machine. *Corona #2: Solar Eclipse* was not the first machine quilted quilt to win a Best of Show award on a national level. Six months earlier, this was achieved at the Houston International Quilt Festival by another quilt but somehow slid under the gossip radar. The backlash heard round the world was caused mainly by the traditional location of the quilt show, the traditional style of the show itself, and quilters who were not ready for change. Caryl took those first punches that thousands of machine quilters would have to endure in the next decade, myself included.

MAGIC CARPET (78" x 83")

*T*his is one of the first quilts that I envisioned with free-hand trapunto. All the motifs are original designs. Other trapuntoed areas on the quilt are freehand. Some of the motifs are stitched with metallic thread. The rest of the quilt is quilted with poly embroidery thread. The hand appliqué on this quilt is all original design by Cheri Meineke-Johnson. Cheri fussy cuts all the motifs from one fabric (which is on the back of the quilt), pieces them together and then hand appliqués them onto one piece of fabric. After *Magic Carpet* was quilted, Cheri applied over 9300 Swarovski crystals to the quilt, a technique that has become her trademark.

~ Linda V. Taylor with Cheri Meineke-Johnson (hand appliqué and design)

AWARDS: Dallas Quilt Celebration: Master's Blue Ribbon and Merit Quilting Award, 2001
MQS: Best of Show, 2001
International Quilt Festival: First Place Ribbon, 2001
NQA: Honorable mention, 2001
QTQ: 1st Place, 2002

This quilt appeared in the quilt show world in 2001 and for a year, we watched as it took the blue ribbon in every show it entered! One reason it did well was the new trend towards crystals. At the time this was a very new embellishment and exciting for judges to see. Another reason it was so successful was that both the piecing and the quilting designs were unique and they complemented each other well.

TIPS TO PREPARE YOUR QUILT FOR SHOW

BLOCKING A QUILT FOR SHOW AND CLEANING IT UP

Blocking a quilt is done before the binding is sewn on. Blocking ensures that your quilt will hang flat and straight on the rod and drape at the show. See the chapter on blocking (p. 38-41) and the enclosed DVD to see how this is done. When you are done with the blocking, and have placed the binding, sleeve and label onto the quilt, it is time to check for stray hanging threads or dog/cat hair and get rid of them. Make sure you look at your quilt at eye level—this will be the area of the quilt that a judge will get closest to. Make sure your binding at eye level is excellent on both sides. This is where they will flip the quilt over to check on your binding skill.

SLEEVES

Most shows have an expectation of where sleeves should be placed. Each show is different in terms of how the quilt hangs. You don't want the quilt hanging on the show floor. Check the entry form for the show's sleeve requirements before it goes to the show. If your quilt does not have a sleeve, you are immediately disqualified from the show. When sewing your sleeve onto the quilt, make sure the sleeve is not visible when your quilt is hanging. (See p. 42-43 and the included DVD for sleeve instructions.)

PHOTOGRAPHY AND THE JURYING PROCESS

Before the judges ever see your quilt, you will first have to enter the quilt in the show. All shows are different in terms of how they accept quilts into the show. Some show committees will sit down as a group and "jury" the quilts into the show with slides or transparencies. Other shows will accept a digital photograph of the quilt with entry forms.

Smaller shows do not jury in quilts, and will not reject any quilt but will want a photo of the quilt with your entry form for identification. You will need to get your quilt shot by a professional photographer if you plan on entering the quilt in different quilt shows. Doing it yourself is not always as professional as having it shot in a studio. Some shows will want two shots of the quilt to prove to them that it is finished. The photographer will be able to get a full size view (showing the binding) and a close up. They will be able to crop the photo so it looks its very best. The photographer can provide you with a CD-ROM of your quilts for a website or provide you with slides for quilt shows. The high resolution photography will show the quilting well and give a show committee more reason to jury your quilt into the show. If they cannot see the quilting, your quilt will not be accepted. The juried shows are looking for the "not so great" quilts. This means they will most likely eliminate the tied quilts, the cheater panel quilts, T-shirt quilts that do not look well made, quilts without sleeves, etc. Jury committees have a tough job and they only have so many spots in the show. Some quilts will make it in the show because the photography is very well done. If you have put hundreds of hours of work into this quilt, it's a good investment to use a professional photographer to create a record of your quilt.

FOLDING

The best way of folding the quilt to prepare for being shipped to a show is to fold the quilt in rectangles (length wise) so gravity will do its job to straighten out the quilt when it hangs on the rod. Some people scrunch the quilt into a ball and ship it that way. (See image on right.) This method isn't universal and seems kind of shocking. The theory is that bundling the quilt up in a messy ball will help the quilt from having a memory of fold lines. But in reality a messy ball can create many, many messy fold lines. Remember, that quilt has been in a cardboard box for a while. Although rolling your quilt and shipping it in a tube sounds like the best way to avoid fold lines, quilt shows do not prefer this method as shipping the quilts back can become complicated. Some quilters prefer to hand deliver and pick up their quilts, avoiding the issue of shipping altogether. If you have to ship your quilt, one suggestion to avoid fold lines is to place wads of tissue paper inside the folds for shipping. When the judge is looking at the quilt, you do not want fold lines to distract them. Major shows steam out the fold lines once the quilt is hung, but most shows do not.

How to Ship the Quilt to the Show

When sending your quilt to a quilt show, I suggest you insure it with the United States Postal Service. Most quilts are considered "irreplaceable" and will not be covered by most carriers. In a nutshell, they will not be covered if you ship them even if you have paid the insurance. The United States Postal Service will cover your items if the quilt is damaged while it is in their care. See the special appraisal article by Jean Carlton, who is an AQS Certified Quilt Appraiser, to understand more about replacement value of your quilt and how

much insurance you will want to have on the quilt. If your quilt is accepted or juried into a show, you will get a letter of congratulations. The letter will also tell you where your quilt should go, how it should go and when you will get it back. Most shows want you to place your quilt in a pillow case, then in a clear, plastic bag marked with your information. Some shows will provide you with identification tags. Each show has different requirements, but generally you ship the quilt about 2 or more weeks before the show opens so it arrives in plenty of time. Each show will also have a drop off location for quilters who prefer to hand deliver their quilts.

Appraisal/What can add to the value of a quilt?

I spoke to Jean Carlton, an AQS Certified Quilt Appraiser about appraisals and what criteria she looks for when making the appraisal. There are so many components to the appraisal system that I asked her to write an article for this book. See "Protect Your Show Quilts" by Jean Carlton on pages 48-49. Below, is a short list of what's important for adding value.

Ribbons, special honors or invitationals. (Be sure to keep good records and tell your appraiser about winning awards. Awards, especially at the larger venues, will increase the quilt's value. Also, they are part of the full history of your piece and should be included on your appraisal document.)

Publications of your quilt, patterns, or articles

Being juried into a major show such as Houston, Paducah, and Chicago

Quiltmaker's recognition in the quilt world

Specialty fabrics or embellishments used in its construction

Quality of construction and workmanship

Graphic appeal

Quiltmaker's record of sales (if applicable)

BLOCKING & SLEEVES

*B*locking is a process that ensures that your quilt will hang perfectly flat. You want your quilt to hang straight on the rod in competition because points are taken away for a wavy quilt. Blocking a quilt requires getting it wet, so make sure your fabrics have been pre-washed to avoid bleeding. You will have to decide if you want to block your quilt on the wall or the floor. Some people use a design wall for blocking, but I find it easier to block a quilt on the floor, especially bigger quilts. The supplies you will need are: measuring tape, stick pins, a sheet, rulers and 2 sheets of foam insulation board. Get the thickest insulation board available so your pins will stay put.

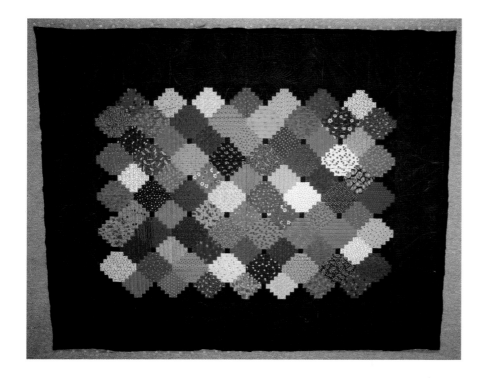

*T*his quilt needs to be blocked so the quilt will hang well in competition.* The quilting designs are still visible, marked in chalk pencil. The quilt has not been bound or trimmed. The markings need to be removed by washing the quilt. Since washing is the first step in blocking, when I submerge the quilt to remove the markings, I am also preparing the quilt for blocking.

*T*his quilt is still damp from being washed and it is ready to be blocked. The markings in the border are gone and some shrinking has begun to wave the edges. Another bonus to washing the quilt is that the ditch quilting in the log cabin blocks becomes beautifully antiqued.

*This is Kris Mattson's quilt. Look for her quilt spread on pages 44-45.

*H*ere is what the foam insulation board looks like. You can find foam insulation board at hardware stores, home improvement stores or lumber yards. Once you get it home from the store, you will need a place to store it.

*F*or a larger quilt, you will need two boards, butted up next to each other on the floor.

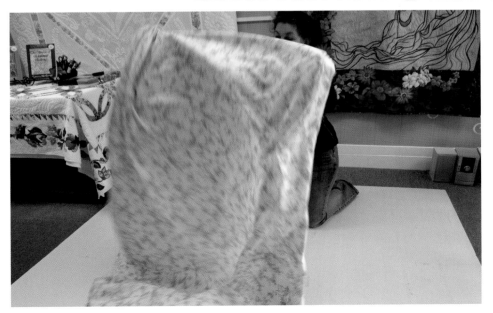

I recommend using a sheet to cover the insulation boards so you have a clean surface to place the wet quilt on.

$\mathcal{L}$ay the damp quilt on top of the sheet. I take off my shoes at this point as I will be crawling around on top of the quilt. You will need pins, a tape measure, rulers, and a friend. You can use a ruler at this point to flatten out any ripples in the quilt by gently sweeping them towards the edges.

$\mathcal{W}$ith your buddy, find the centers of the quilt's borders, determine the length of the washed quilt, stretch the quilt back to it's original size and place a pin on each side.

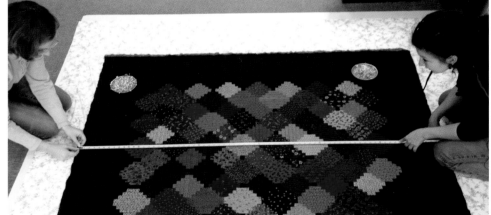

$\mathcal{N}$ext, find the centers of the quilt's side borders, stretch the quilt back to it's original size, place your pins and then start to place pins every ½ inch around the border.

KAREN'S TIPS:

$\mathcal{Y}$ou don't have to measure every pin. Place about 6 pins, then measure again.

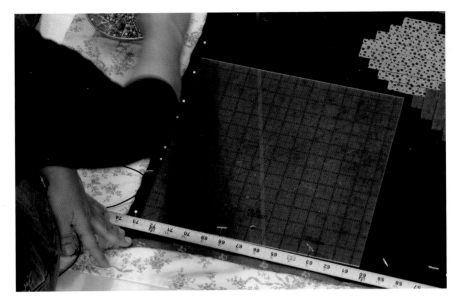

*U*sing a quilt square in the corner will help you pin the corner perfectly square and flat.

KAREN'S TIPS:

*M*ake sure to place the pins in the binding area, not through the quilt top where they may rust and discolor the quilt top.

*O*nce all the pins are in place, the quilt needs to dry flat. You may use fans to speed the process if you would like. Keep the animals away from this space until your quilt is dry. After the quilt is dry it will retain this flat memory and will hang straight on the rod until it gets washed again.

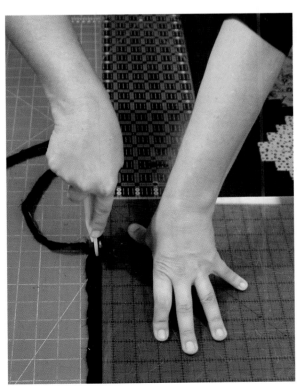

*A*fter the quilt is dry, remove the pins to prepare for the trimming process.

*Y*ou will need a long ruler for the borders and a square for the corners in order to trim the quilt edges accurately.

*W*hen you are done trimming, the quilt will be ready for a sleeve.

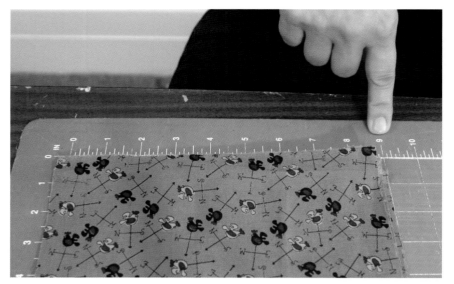

Generally, sleeves are cut at 9 inches by the length of the shortest side of the quilt. Measure your quilt top first - if the quilt is 60 inches x 68 inches, your sleeve should be cut at 9 inches by 59 inches. This will give you a half inch of leeway from each side of the binding.

I like to press the ends of the sleeve in, and then run a stitch across the fold to secure the edges from fraying in the future.

Fold the sleeve in half lengthwise and sew a seam down the length of the sleeve, making a tube.

Open the seam and press it. The side with the seam is going to be facing the quilt backing and will not be seen.

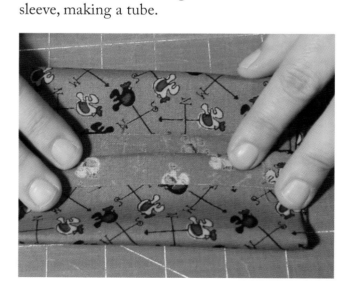

Now take your sleeve and pin it in place at the top of the back of the quilt. Don't pin it right at the top—you need to leave room for the sleeve to move when the quilt is hanging on the rod. Pin the top of your sleeve about 2 inches from where the top of the quilt will be once your binding is finished. Start pinning the sleeve from the center and work your way out.

After the top edge of your sleeve is sewn on, you have to create some room in the sleeve for the rod. Do not sew your sleeve flat against the quilt backing. You want your sleeve to be like a tube. Slide the sleeve up 1 inch from the bottom of the edge of the sleeve. You can pin the fold in place while you sew it down by hand. If you do not do this step, your sleeve will be so tight that the hanging rod will create a bulge in the front of your quilt when it's hanging in a show.

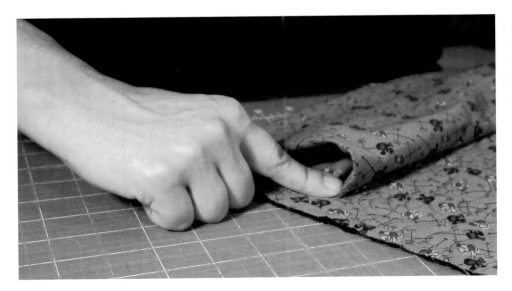

After you sew the length of the sleeve, you will see that you have created a tube and you have room for the rod.

Your next step is binding. However, I am not an expert in this area so I recommend that you either take a class or buy a book on binding. There are a variety of books and classes available on this topic.

ONE STEP AT A TIME (71" x 59")

I pieced this quilt and it was beautifully quilted by Karen McTavish. The quilt was pieced in the winter of 2002-2003. I was inspired by a quilt that had been featured in a *Fons and Porter* issue. *One Step at a Time* was pieced with love and patience for my Mom who had been diagnosed with Alzheimer's earlier that year. Thank you to Karen for making my quilt so stunning, my family for always encouraging me to try and to my Mom for passing on a gift. ~ *Anita Kris Mattson*

$\mathcal{T}$his quilt was a joy to quilt for Kris. When I first saw this quilt I noticed the excellent piecing and the plain black borders. I knew immediately that I could make this into something to compete with. The borders designs are all original and hand drawn directly to the quilt top. Judges will notice that the borders are original and as long as my stitches are consistent and my tension is in good shape, we should be able to compete with this quilt. Watch the included DVD to see exactly how I blocked this quilt. The binding and piping were done by Patricia Harrison of Exeter, Rhode Island. Because three people worked on this quilt (piecing, quilting and binding) we will enter the quilt in a group category.

BUTTERFLIES IN MY GARDEN
(90" x 114")

Kathy Shier does some of the most beautiful appliqué I have ever seen. Her stitches are so tiny and fine that I get a headache even thinking about trying to duplicate them. When she brought this stunning quilt to me for quilting, I was both flattered by the trust she was placing in me, and intimidated as all-get-out at the mere thought of trying to come up with a quilting design that would live up to her exquisite handwork.

My first impression of the quilt was of movement. The flowers all seemed to be dancing in an unseen wind, and my goal was to enhance and reinforce this impression. By using the McTavishing technique as an overall design, I feel that I was able to accomplish this goal. The quilting adds the effect of air currents moving through the quilt and among the flowers, and at the same time manages to fade into the background and let the beautiful appliqué sing. From the moment I laid eyes on this quilt, I knew it would go far, and my job would be to just stay out of the way and let the quilt have the limelight.

The quilting design was totally freehand, and took approximately 70 hours of actual machine quilting time, with another 30 hours spent standing and staring blankly while wondering what on earth to do next. In retrospect, I wish I had done some cutaway trapunto, as I think the quilt would have been further enhanced by this technique, but done is good. The judges seem to have been happy with the finished result, and gave it very good scores in workmanship, design, use of color, and choice of quilting design.

– Kim Brunner with Kathy Shier (piecing and appliqué)

AWARDS: Innovations: First Place, 2003
MQX: First Place, 2004
MQS: Teacher's Ribbon, 2004
Dakota County Fair: First Place, 2004
QOTW: Honorable Mention, 2004
Minnesota Quilters State Quilt Show: First Place, 2004

Nothing works better in show than combining contemporary appliqué with McTavishing. This accomplishes two things: it allows the appliqué to pop up and the background to lay flat. Judges are completely bored with stippling and want to see something new and exciting. Today's trends in quilting tell us to be as creative as possible. Staying away from the tried and true is a safe bet. It is still important to stitch in the ditch around the appliqué. If you choose not to stitch in the ditch, you are taking a giant short cut and your ribbon may turn into an honorable mention instead of a first place.

PROTECT YOUR SHOW QUILTS

FACTS ABOUT QUILT APPRAISALS
by Jean Carlton,
Minnesota Quilt
Appraiser

Certified by the American Quilter's Society (AQS)

Having a written appraisal done for your show quilt by a qualified quilt appraiser is a very important step. It will include a complete description of your quilt, rating its workmanship and condition, recording any history about its creation and arriving at a replacement value. Your quilt is a valuable textile. In addition to the cost of your fabrics and other supplies used in its creation, you have invested your time and creativity as well. Entering your quilt in a show does involve risks during shipping and while on display. No one likes to think about it but quilts do get damaged or lost sometimes. Bad things *do* sometimes happen to good quilts...

SHIPPING
The replacement value determined by your appraiser allows you to properly insure your quilt for shipping. Should the unthinkable happen, you will be much more likely to get proper reimbursement. The United States Postal Service and other private shipping companies will sell you insurance in any amount, but they often do not inform you that should a claim be made you will be asked to provide proof of the value of the shipped item. Purchasing a specific amount of insurance does not guarantee you reimbursement in that amount. A receipt is the preferred proof. But, as quilt makers we do not typically have receipts for the fabrics, batting, thread and other components of our quilts. Even having receipts for the materials involved in making a specific quilt does not take into account the time involved with the design and construction of the quilt which *is* included in determining the replacement cost of a newly made quilt.

SHOW INSURANCE
Most shows insure the quilts in their care up to a specific amount. If you want your quilt insured for more than that amount while exhibited, you may be asked to include a copy of an appraisal by a certified appraiser with your registration.

Having your quilt appraised for replacement value can save you much grief and give you peace of mind while it is being shipped and exhibited to the public and also serves to protect you in the event of damage or theft once it's home again.

Additional Tips to Protect Your Quilt

Labels

Your show quilt will, of course, be labeled clearly on the back with your name, address, city, state, zip code and phone number. Think about applying the label BEFORE quilting for added security as the label will be difficult to remove. You can take extra precaution by using a fine permanent pen to write your name inside the seam allowance in one corner before completing the last step of the binding. Put it in the corner where the label is attached. If there is ever any question about quilt ownership, your proof is in the binding!

Photos

Be sure to photograph your quilt. Include a full view and a close up or two. Flip over one corner and take a photo to show the backing and binding. Be sure to have someone take a photo of you with the quilt, also.

Other Types of Appraisals

This article discusses the type of appraisal which would be required to determine *an insurance replacement value* for your quilt. Other types of appraisals are available to determine fair market value when selling or donating a quilt or if a value needs to be determined for estate or divorce settlements.

Contact Jean at QuiltsEtc@comcast.net with questions. For further information about quilt appraisals or to find an appraiser in your area who has been certified by the American Quilter's Society, go to their website, www.americanquilter.com, where there is a link to the Appraiser List, or go to www.quiltappraisers.org, the site of the Professional Association of Quilt Appraisers (PAAQT). Appraisers on this site are also AQS Certified. Both sites allow you to search by state or name of appraiser.

NEW DAWN
(78" x 63")

*T*his is one of a series of quilts about birds as symbols of freedom and the joy of life. It was made in the year 2000 especially to celebrate the dawning of the new millennium. I chose the mythical Phoenix as a symbol of leaving behind the old and beginning anew. To me the Phoenix is a symbol of the ability of life and beauty to rise out of decay and destruction. The transition to a new millennium gave us a reason to think about what was good about the old millennium, and what we would like to change. It gave us a chance to focus our visions and make new and positive choices for ourselves and for our world.

Since the Phoenix is a mythical bird and there are no photographs of it, the bird in this quilt is entirely a product of my imagination. The design evolved over a period of several months. I spent days drawing wing feathers and heads of real birds to get the feeling of how feathers work together, and how they relate to the rest of a bird. My Phoenix is a composite of many different elements from many different birds. Since the wings form a perfect circle (symbol of wholeness) the feathers had to be designed to fit the contour of this geometric shape. A spiral (symbol of new growth and reemergence) of "flying geese" emerges from the mouth of the Phoenix. They are made from a gradation of rainbow colors, symbolizing light and the energy of life.

The Phoenix itself is made from a variety of iridescent and metallic fabrics. The long tail is intertwined with the flames, which have consumed the old Phoenix, and from which the new Phoenix is rising. As the Phoenix rises from the flames, it is about to fly through a portal of black, white and grey, toward clear skies and unlimited possibilities beyond. In the corners of the portal are a golden sun and a fire colored sun. These represent energy that can be either nurturing or destructive. Our choice. ~ *Caryl Bryer Fallert*

AWARDS:
Quilt Festival: Millennium Quilt Contest 2000 (and traveling)
Solo Exhibition: Caryl Bryer Fallert - A Sense of Wonder, Burlington Arts Center, Ontario 2001
Thirty Distinguished Quiltmakers in the World: Tokyo, Japan 2002
QTQ: Best Domestic Machine Quilting 2002
Solo Exhibition: Little White School Museum, Oswego, IL 2003
AQS 20th Anniversary: Best of Show Exhibit, MAQS 2004
Solo Exhibition: Evolving Styles - 20 Years of Color & Design, LaConner Quilt Museum, WA 2005
Quilting by the Lake: Faculty Exhibition, Morrisville, NY 2005
Jinny Beyer Quilting Seminar: Faculty Exhibition, Hilton Head Island, NC 2006
National Quilting Association Show (invitational): Columbus, OH 2006

Caryl's innovative work sets this quilt apart from the more traditional quilts we tend to see in quilting competition. The eye of the Phoenix is made of laser foil, and changes color as the viewer moves from side to side. You don't see that in the quilting world regularly! Original quilts like *New Dawn* start as hand drawings and end in a magnificent quilt. This shows a judge that the Quiltmaker has "excellence and knowledge in construction." This is a term that judges will use when they know that a quilt is a "one of a kind" quilt. Caryl had to figure out all the piecing placement and construction issues herself. No pattern help or piecing directions of any kind was used to help create this quilt.

SCARLET SERENADE (97" x 97")

AWARDS: IQA: Best of Show, 2005
          AQS: Best of Show, 2006
          AQS: 1st Place Longarm Machine Workmanship, 2006
          MQS: Best of Show, 2006

*T*his quilt was made over a four year period and features a hand corded border. The quilt was appraised in 2006 for a value of $9,500. This quilt is the first longarm machine quilted quilt to win a "Best of Show" on an international level. ~ *Sharon Schamber*

*T*his quilt shows Sharon's many years of teaching, quilting and her expertise in her craft. She is a well known instructor and is currently the most exciting quilter on the circuit. She will forever be known as the quilter who took the very first "Best of Show" at an International show using a longarm quilting machine. This is ground breaking for the longarm world and we all felt like we won when *Scarlet Serenade* took Best of Show at the Houston International Quilt Show in 2005.

SEDONA ROSE (105" x 110")

*T*his piece was machine quilted on a longarm using my "Piec-lique" technique. The quilt has over 100,000 Swarovski crystals heat set on the back of it. In 2006 it was appraised at $12,000 and is now the property of the Museum of American Quilters Society in Paducah, Kentucky.

~Sharon Schamber

AWARDS: AQS: Best of Show (Purchase Award), 2006

Sharon's quilt is two sided. The dense background fillers, quilted on a longarm quilting machine, are perfectly placed and all the motifs are her originals. Her use of black bobbin thread on butterscotch backing fabric created a secondary masterpiece. To add to the impact she applied over 130,000 crystals to the back of the quilt, by hand, over a six week period. If you could get through the crowds surrounding this Best of Show quilt, you might be one of the lucky ones to see the back of the quilt. Enjoying the front of the quilt is enough to make anyone feel thrilled to see it in person, but to view the back of this quilt is a one of a kind experience. The distinctive binding, based on her background as a wedding dress maker, is something the quilt world has never seen before. She also brought back the use of DMC cotton embroidery thread.

COMMON COMMENTS
MADE BY JUDGES TO THE AUTHOR

*H*ere is a list of actual comments I have received from judges—in their own words! Some of it is easy to take, like the positive comments, but sometimes the truth hurts. Some of the comments are ambiguous and vague. Sometimes the comments are a direct hit and pull no punches. We look to the critique to help us be better quilters. If we didn't look at the critique as a tool to better ourselves, we would all be depressed and never quilt again.

"Quilting motifs well chosen for both design and coverage of quilt surface."

"Border quilting motif should be spaced so binding does not cover it."

"Quilting designs well planned to show off blocks."

"Stops and starts very visible on the backing."

"Well placed quilting designs and borders."

"Watch stitch length consistency."

"Good thread color choices."

"Contrasting thread not effective."

"Avoid overlapping of quilt lines."

"Watch tension control in some areas."

"Good backtracking control."

"Visible stops and starts."

"Quilting effective."

"Very Effective Quilting."

"Binding technique needs improvement."

"Strive for consistent straight crosshatching."

"Invisible thread is a good idea around appliqué."

"Quilt does not hang straight."

"Trapunto adds interest."

"Feather filler very well done."

"Quilting density becomes a serious issue."

"Background quilting with Trapunto is beautiful."

And my favorite comment from Kaye England:

"This machine quilter appears to have had way too much fun quilting this quilt."

WHOLECLOTH AND PATIENCE (78" x 100")

AWARDS: Machine Quilters Showcase: 1st Place, Wholecloth, 2001
Minnesota State Fair: Best Machine Quilting, 2001
Minnesota State Fair: 1st Place, Wholecloth, 2001
Quilting the Quilt: 3rd Place, Wholecloth Large, 2002

*T*his was my first attempt at a wholecloth quilt. I was inspired by the wholecloth quilters in Kalona, Iowa. Little did they know the monster they created when I came to town! I took the plain, white fabric to a quilting retreat, along with my theme border (purchased in Kalona) and my stencil stash. The off-white, 80/20 cotton-poly, trapunto batting created subtle contrast between the trapunto and the background. The main batting of this quilt is Quilters Dream Poly; it drapes really well, helps reduce fold lines, doesn't take a bleed and doesn't shrink. I don't think I would have ever finished my first wholecloth if my mother had not caught me putting it away. ~ *Karen McTavish*

GENERAL SUGGESTIONS
FOR WORKING ON YOUR SHOW QUILT

Remember to stitch in the ditch at all times. (Not stitching in the ditch is a short cut. Judges will notice and it will create a distraction.)

Trapunto should be used in the appliqué if you are going for a formal traditional look.

Avoid stippling and micro-stippling. This trend is over and judges are uninterested in this heavy background filler.

Large meandering should be avoided altogether.

Using original designs from your hand drawings or custom/modified motifs always helps a quilt to be innovative and unique.

Avoid entering a quilt made from a kit as judges are looking for original work.

Use a stitch regulated machine if possible.

If you are crosshatching, the crosshatching should not be larger than 1 inch wide. Crosshatching trends are currently very small – ¼ inch to ½ inch is most common.

Avoid short cuts at all costs. Judges know what is easy and what is difficult.

Credibility will be earned for difficult techniques.

Don't wing it when it comes to designing the quilting. Have a well thought out design plan.

Some judges want to see "quilted to death" quilts while others feel that the quilting trend of heavy quilting causes the quilt to be stiff as a board and feel this style is unsuitable.

Your main batting choice should be a batting that will surrender its fold lines. Wool has a memory and retains fold lines, while poly batting does not.

IRISH CRÈME (92" x 92")

AWARDS: MQS: 2nd Place Theme, 2003
Mid-Atlantic Quilt Festival: 1st Place Traditional, 2004
QOTW: 2 Teachers' Ribbons, 2004

*T*his quilt showcases dark green stars on a cream background. This quilt includes Hobbs' Wool Batting, Superior Threads' Bottom Line and Moda Marble Fabrics. The vase work quilting designs in the corners of the quilt are original hand drawings, drawn on to freezer paper first, and then marked directly on the quilt. My inspiration for the quilting in this quilt came from seeing Diane Gaudynski's work. ~ *Carol A. Selepec*

𝒲hen I first saw this quilt hanging in a show, I immediately thought the quilt used trapunto. But later I discovered that Carol used two full battings instead of using the cut away method. The scalloped edge binding adds further visual impact to the quilt. If this difficult binding technique is within your quilting ability it will appeal to judges. A scalloped edge binding or a corded binding is a quilter's way of "showing off" a little. Adding a complex binding gives you a little bit more credibility with judges as long as it is done very well. Some judges want perfection in difficult techniques. They want to see "expertise in this technique."

BALI BLUES
(84" x 94")

AWARDS:

QOTW: 3rd Place
Traditional Longarm,
2004

I was inspired to make *Bali Blues* after being a little disappointed that the same designs on my previous quilt, *Irish Crème*, didn't pop out enough. I decided to use the cut away trapunto method on *Bali Blues* with a couple layers of different battings to see what that would do to improve the designs. It took 80 hours to cut away all the extra batting but it was worth it. The designs now popped out and the new detail was amazing. I added the red piping to give the quilt a little extra color detail, using Susan Cleveland's piping method. The judges seem to like special extras when it comes to competition pieces. I enjoyed creating the feathered vase designs. *Irish Crème* and *Bali Blues* were both designed so that I could showcase 2 different vase designs— one set of 4 in the center of the quilt and the second set of 4 in the outer corners. I picked blue batiks for the stars and white cotton sateen for the rest of the quilt. I used Warm & White, Quilters Dream Poly and Soft & Bright battings for the trapunto and main batting. I quilted with cotton wrapped poly thread and The Bottom Line. ~ *Carol A. Selepec*

*T*his is a comparison quilt to *Irish Crème.* How often to we see comparison quilts? Not very often. Carol used cut-away trapunto this time instead of faux trapunto and avoided wool batting. Again, being inspired by Diane Gaudynski's feather work, Carol drew all her original feather plumes and vases on freezer paper then transferred the drawings directly to her quilt top. Judges love originality in quilting motifs and little extra touches such as piping in the binding, add to the complexity of the quilt. We are trying to show off where we can and the binding is the perfect place to add a little bit of zip to the piece. When I see Carol's signature style of quilting, I don't even have to look at the name tag to know she was the one who created it.

FIXING PROBLEM AREAS IN SHOW QUILTS

I have fixed problems with a quilt based on a judge's critique many times. All the professional quiltmakers will do this. It is very common to get your first critique, agree with the judges and have no choice but to fix the problem. After you fix the problem areas of the quilt, show it again and see how your work pays off. Linda McCuean, Quilting Judge, National Award Winning Quilter and Instructor shares her story on what she did when a judge critiqued her quilt, *Jubilee*, which is featured following this commentary.

JUBILEE

"*W*hen I was designing *Jubilee*, my goal was to create a winning quilt—one that represented my very best work at that time in both design and workmanship. I wanted a striking visual impact in a design that was reminiscent of the antique red and green appliqué quilts that I so admire, with lots of open spaces for elaborate trapunto and quilting. I wanted a quilt that I could send out into the national level shows to test the waters and see how my work held up in stiffer competition.

"*Jubilee's* show career started off with a bang. It won Best of Show at Machine Quilter's Showcase in Springfield, IL, followed by Best of Show at Quilting the Quilt in Duluth, MN. These 2 wins were definitely the high point of my career as a longarm quilter.

"When *Jubilee* came home from the first show, I couldn't wait to read the judging critique. As I expected, the only negative comment was on the slight ripple of the outside edges. I knew this was because there was less quilting in the sawtooth border triangles, and that I could correct it by re-blocking and applying the binding more carefully. So I sat down with the quilt that had just been deemed Best of Show, and carefully picked off the ¼" binding and ⅛" piping. It was well worth the effort as *Jubilee* has gone on to win 8 Best of Show awards, as well as the AQS Gammill Longarm Quilting award, and numerous machine quilting awards.

"It still amazes me when people come up to me at shows and know who I am because of my quilts. I thank God daily for this gift He has given me to work with my hands using simple textiles to fashion something of beauty that can bring joy to so many." ~ *Linda McCuean*

JUBILEE (79" x 81")

*A*ntique red and green appliqué quilts with lots of fancy quilting are my very favorite type of quilts, but I know I don't have enough time – or perseverance – to do all that hand quilting! So my answer is to re-create that beauty in an all machine made reproduction of that style. I employed today's techniques of machine appliqué, foundation piecing, trapunto, and machine quilting to replicate the wonderful handwork of our quilting ancestors. This quilt brought together the very best of my abilities at that point in time. *Jubilee* has had a long and very successful show career. *Jubilee* also instilled in me the desire to make each quilt in some way better than the one before.

~ *Linda McCuean*

Linda McCuean is an award winning quilter and a quilt judge. Linda's judging style is similar to her quilting style in respect to tradition. Linda's quilts are very traditional and generally combine appliqué and trapunto. Her judging reputation shows a great respect for the hand quilter. This is also mirrored in her work. Her quilts have changed the face of longarm quilting by smashing the "cookie cutter" label that is attached to many machine quilters.

AWARDS:
MQS: Best of Show, 2002
QTQ: Best of Show, 2002
Mid Atlantic Quilt Festival: 1st Place Traditional, 2003
Quilter's Heritage Celebration:
        Fairfield Workmanship Award, 2003
AQS: Gammill Longarm Machine Quilting Award, 2003
Quilt Odyssey: 1st Place Mixed Techniques, 2003
Road to California: Best of Show, 2004
NQA: Best Machine Quilting, 2004
NQA: Best of Show, 2004
Rockome Gardens: Best of Show, 2005

BURYING YOUR THREADS

WHY IT'S IMPORTANT

I spoke with Pepper Cory, one of the top judges in the quilting world, regarding her thoughts on quilting competition. I have followed her career for years and she has judged many of my quilts in several different shows. The biggest problem area I would see on my quilting critiques from Pepper would always say, "Watch your stops and starts." This is a standard comment that many judges will make to machine quilters who do not bury the tails of their threads. Pepper has a strong hand quilting background and has accepted machine quilting fully as part of today's quiltmaking. As I followed her style of judging, I became aware that she holds a great amount of respect for the traditional and for a well constructed quilt. Her critiques are direct and fair, in my experience, when she judges my quilts. My only hope was that she would miraculously overlook my problem areas. It's nice to live in optimism, if only for a brief moment!

Over the years Pepper has seen quilting trends come and go. She was judging when machine quilted quilts were just starting to peek into competition. As a hand quilting authority, she became more creditable as a judge when she embraced machine quilting, instead of rejecting it. Her judging ability tends to be "dead on" accurate with the problems of the quilt. I am not going to lie—it is painful to hear the truth. But if you can fix the problems, you'll do better at the next show.

One of the biggest issues that I struggle with in my own quilting is burying threads. At the time this book was written, you could see me literally standing "on the fence" in regard to burying the threads. Some judges really care about this issue, some do not, but the current trend in quilt shows is that it is important to most judges in general. First ask yourself, "Do I have what it takes to be like a hand quilter and bury my thread tails with a needle to hide my stop and starts or should I just knot 'em and then clip 'em?" or "Am I really ready to do such time consuming and tedious work?" I needed to talk to Pepper Cory.

I spoke at length with Pepper about why burying threads is important to her. For Pepper, when focusing on the quilting of the quilt (not the piecing) visible stops and starts (or knots) are the first thing she sees. A quilt with good quilting construction will have the threads buried. The quilting should be well planned and thought out. The quilting should compliment the top—not over or under-whelm it. There should be a good collaboration between the piecer and the quilter; they should create the quilt together. But overall, if there are visible starts and stops in the stitching and thread tails are not buried, Pepper feels these distract from the work. This distraction will be the deal breaker. Maybe not a deal breaker in terms of a 1st Place ribbon or an Honorable Mention ribbon but more along the lines of being juried into the show and not ribboning at all.

My standard answer when the question, "Do you bury your threads?" comes up, would be, "The pain factor is not high enough yet." When I spoke to Pepper, her word "distraction" was a light bulb moment for me. When I have judged quilts at shows, I will get hung up on a "distraction" too. If I see a drag on a quilt in competition (this is a term used when you pick up your needle and move, or drag, over to another area of the quilt, and continue quilting, then snip off the thread on the top and backing without securing the tails) it is a huge distraction for me and I move on to another quilt. Another distraction for me would be inconsistent stitches. To avoid creating these kinds of distractions, I would need to enter a flawless quilt. I can achieve flawless if I make the commitment and have the determination.

So I have changed my tune somewhat when I think of burying my threads at my stops and starts. Now I just have to remember to keep my hand needle handy and bury my quilting threads instead of clipping them. Is winning awards easy? Nothing is easy. What doesn't kill you makes you an award winning quilter.

"Actually the needle I prefer for tail-burying is a gold-headed embroidery needle. This gold-headed needle, plus it being embroidery-size, is easier to see—a constant reminder to bury your thread tails. The needle should be sharp and rust-free. Often quilters keep those utility needles for years. Pitch 'em! Get a good quality English embroidery needle and when it's not parked on the side of your quilt top, keep it in a pin cushion." ~ *Pepper Cory*

Pepper Cory - Quilting Judge,
Author and Quiltmaker

How to Bury your Threads

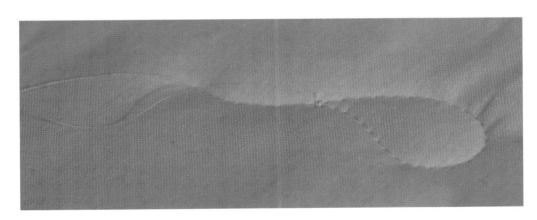

To start, bring the bobbin thread up to the top of the quilt to join the top thread, as shown. Make sure your tails are long enough for threading onto the embroidery needle.

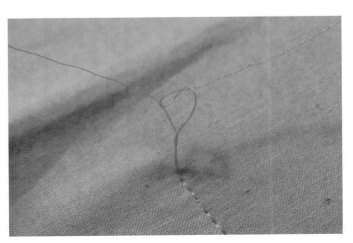

Before you thread your needle, tie your tails in a simple knot on your quilt top.

Tie it down tight.

Now thread your two tails into the eye of the needle. With embroidery needles, you can actually "pop" the thread through the needle at the top if you can't see the entrance. See the "H" that appears at the top of the needle? That spot has an opening to pop the thread down into the hole.

Direct your needle through the entrance of the knot. Do not go through the layers of the quilt—just inch along the underside of the quilt top. Travel about an inch away from the knot.

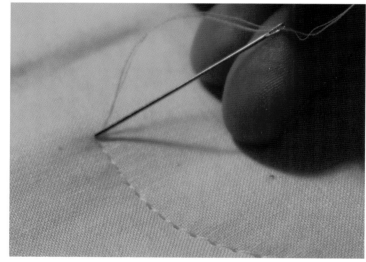

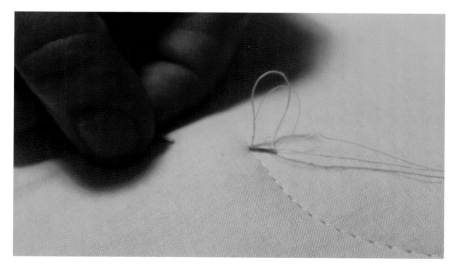

Pull your needle back through the top.

*W*ith some force, but not too much, pop the knot in between the top and batting layers of the quilt.

*N*ow you can snip off the ends of your thread. Your buried knot and tail will live under your quilt top in the batting layer.

*B*urying your threads results in a very clean look to your quilting design.

Shows, Categories and Ethics

Finding a Quilt Show

There are so many quilt shows in the United States today that your quilt could be on the road for two years and never hit the same show twice. You can find quilt shows in the back of most quilting magazines by dates and locations or by simply going on-line and entering "Quilt Shows" in a search engine.

There are guild, local, state-wide, national and international shows. Generally, you start showing your quilt on a local or state-wide level and if it does well, you continue on to a national or international level. Joining a local quilting guild in your area will expose you to the quilting circuit, as guilds generally volunteer to organize and run their annual quilt shows. You can volunteer to hang or take down quilts in the show or to be a "white glove person."

On the day you have placed the last stitch into the quilt, your quilt's internal stop watch will start running. You only have two years to show your quilt, and then it will no longer qualify for most national quilt shows. You cannot put off entering your quilt because in the quilt world, two years goes pretty fast. If the show is in April, your paperwork should have been sent in to the show in January. Having your paperwork done and sent in months before the show gives you the opportunity to make travel plans to go see your quilt in the show once you know it is accepted. Sometimes getting juried into a show at all is worth the trip. If I am accepted into a juried show, that's usually enough to make me happy. If I have no expectations of the quilt, I will never be disappointed with the outcome.

Category Requirements

Every show has different categories, rules and requirements. There are many different categories in which to enter your quilt at a quilt show and finding the right category is important. Some shows base their categories on size. For example, some shows will categorize a wall quilt as any quilt smaller than 60" x 60" while other shows base their categories on technique.

To start with, figure out if you are in a miniature, wall or large category. You will need to know the exact measurement of your quilt before you fill out your paperwork for the entry. Next, determine if your quilt is a single entry, two-person entry or group entry. How many people were involved in helping you with your quilt? Are you considered amateur or professional? Then, decide if your quilt is traditional or contemporary. Is it a pictorial or art quilt? Or did you make it for a specific challenge category? Shows with theme

or challenge categories often have specific fabric requirements. Each show will walk you through the process of figuring out the different category requirements.

I have run into problems entering my machine quilted wholecloth quilts at shows. Some shows have a hand-quilting category where the requirements are "two pieces of fabric, front and back, which have no other element but quilting." This means "wholecloth" but since my quilts are machine quilted, they do not qualify. Since wholecloth is not pieced, the quilt would be disqualified from a traditional pieced category. A category option to look for at this point is "solitaire" or "first time entrant." Each show you enter requires a process of elimination to find the best possible fit for your quilt. Your chances of ribboning improve if you pick the correct category in which to enter your quilt.

ETHICS AND EXPECTATIONS

If you enter your quilt in a show in a Duo (Two Person) category the show generally awards two ribbons. One ribbon is for the quilter, one for the piecer. The award may also come with a monetary prize. Often, a single check is written out to the owner of the quilt, or to the person who entered the quilt in the show.

It is important to remember that there are two people involved in making a quilt. It is a collaborative effort. The piecer and the quilter should split the prize award; nothing would have been achieved without the other's participation. It's good to conduct yourself in this manner of sharing, so you can continue to have a long relationship with the other party involved and continue to create quilts together without animosity. It's very important to acknowledge all persons who were involved in making the quilt in quilt competitions.

Most quilt shows' awards are monetary with a ribbon, but your quilt could also win a purchase award. Purchase awards mean you are no longer the owner of the quilt and it is forever preserved in a museum. You are also given a very large check for the pain of losing your quilt. Purchase awards are the ultimate goal of most professional quilters who show on a competitive level.

FIRE DRAGON RHAPSODY (61" x 61")

*I*ron grillwork featuring a stylized dragon on a window in downtown Pueblo, CO became the inspiration for this quilt. I scanned a pencil outline into the computer and manipulated it in reverse and mirror image to create the overall design. Using Justin Shults' hand-dyed fabrics, I created the quilt using many machine elements, including bobbin quilting, machine trapunto and a piped binding. Each "Rhapsody" quilt I make features a variety of elements and techniques that are unified in the whole. The quilt is now part of the permanent collection at the Museum of the American Quilter's Society in Paducah, KY. ~ *Ricky Tims*

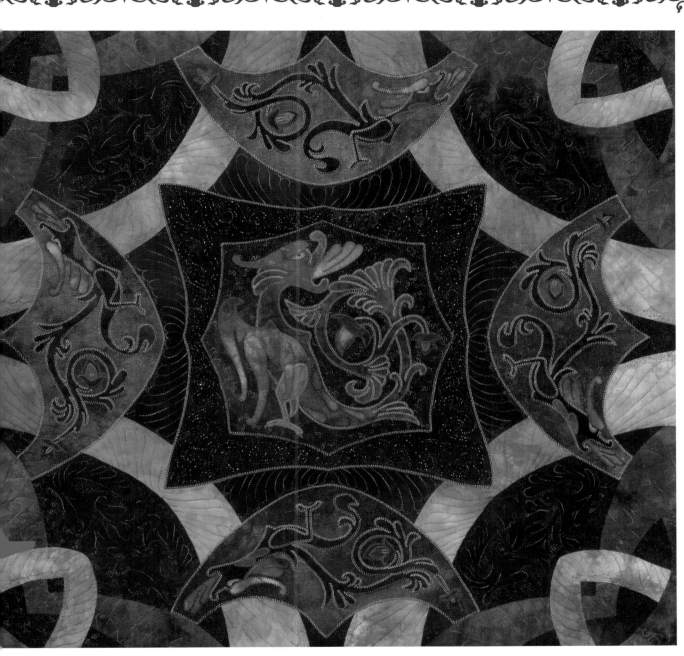

AWARDS: AQS: Best Machine Workmanship, 2006

Fire Dragon has so many different many elements to it, you'll have to pull up a chair and sit for a while to appreciate everything. I really like the brave use of contrasting thread and the tight quilting. From the hand dyed fabrics to the quilt piecing which he designed, to the quilting motifs—this quilt is original from start to finish and is completely Ricky's style. Judges want to see originality and this quilt is a perfect example. The impressive qualities of this quilt resulted in a purchase award.

THE GRANDFATHER (54" x 44")

AWARDS: IQA: 1st Place Ribbon, 2000
IQA: Judges Choice Award, 2000

January 1, 1992, our family was invited to a New Year's celebration in Mali. The party took place on the sandy banks of the Niger River. Shelters to protect everyone from the sun were built out of straw and bamboo. About two hundred people came and celebrated the New Year with music, dance, good food and lots of laughter. A grandfather was there with his granddaughter. He was so loving and gentle with her that I photographed him several times peeling an orange for her. This piece was inspired by my favorite of these photographs. Technique: Hand dye-painted with thickened fiber reactive dyes on cotton fabrics, machine pieced border and machine quilted, Cotton Classic batting.

~ *Hollis Chatelain*

𝒲hat is so amazing about Hollis's style of quilting is that she paints the background first and then starts to quilt. She does not use variegated threads. She uses thread as a pallet for her color choices. For example, every color change you see in her quilt is done using another spool of different colored thread. So if you see a quilted line that changes from tan to brown to black – that's three different times she has had to change her thread color. This means at each color change, she expertly hid the stops and starts to make it look painted or variegated.

REMEMBRANCE
(82" x 80")

A quilt titled *Ivy's Pincushion* made by Bertha Stenge in the 1930's inspired the central medallion of this quilt. The delicate appliqué design allowed lots of open spaces for the extensive trapunto work that I love to include in my quilts. I designed the simple framing border to enclose the open areas, but not compete with the quilting. The picture I had of Bertha's quilt was not clear enough to allow me to duplicate her quilting designs, so my imagination had to take over. I used several line drawings from a Dover copyright free design book and adapted them to create the flowing designs for quilting. I used taupe colored polar fleece for the trapunto batting to shade the stuffed areas. It added just enough color to give a vintage look to the quilt. Polar fleece is wonderful to work with and gives a true color that will not fade or bleed. The variety of background quilting patterns adds a lot of texture and visual interest to the quilt. Over 7000 meters of silk thread were used for the quilting. I spent a lot of time working on this quilt and thinking about the common bond I had with this woman, Bertha Stenge, whom I had never met. She obviously loved designing and creating beautiful quilts, as I do. She made her quilt for a contest, just as I was honoring her design in my quilt for another competition. I also thought of another Bertha, my grandmother, who was not a quilter, but was a strong woman whose independence I have always admired. The name *Remembrance* seemed perfect. ~ *Linda McCuean*

AWARDS: MQS: 1st Place Innovative Custom, 2003
MQS: Viewer's Choice, 2003
Pennsylvania National Quilt Extravaganza: Best of Show, 2003
Quilter's Newsletter Magazine 35th Anniversary Contest:
1st Place Updated Traditional, 2004
Quilt Odyssey: Best Artistry in Longarm Quilting, 2005

*O*ne of the greatest things about Linda's quilts is that she rarely uses commercially made stencils. All her quilting motifs are original designs, with a theme from an inspiration she had. We know judges love originality in quilts, and this is a perfect combination with trapunto and appliqué. As a tradition lover myself, I enjoy seeing Linda's quilts and look forward to seeing her new creations every year.

CACTUS ROSE (73" x 73")

Cactus Rose is truly a collaboration among friends. Claudia Clark Myers designed the paper piecing pattern called *Cactus Rose*. Marilyn Badger pieced it using her favorite desert colors, and Myrna demonstrated her expertise in using hand-held guides with her longarm machine and in filling the spaces with free-motion quilting. Another friend, Heather Purcell of Superior Threads provided the Bottom Line thread for the fine quilting and Razzle Dazzle for the added sparkle in the couching.

~ Myrna Ficken (quilter) with Claudia Clark Myers (designer) and Marilyn Badger (piecer)

Again, Myrna uses the geometric piecing in this quilt to her advantage by adding curves and circles to her quilting motifs. You see more flow and activity with the use of circles in this quilt. A judge will appreciate how each element plays off the other. Myrna's quilt uses some unexpected threads in the ditch which is new and unique to a judge's eye. The end result is a well balanced quilt which uses several original ideas.

AWARDS:

MQS: 1st Place Tools of the Trade, 2006

QOTW: 3rd Place Traditional Longarm, 2006

Road to California: 1st Place Traditional Large, 2007

BIRDS IN PARADISE - FRONT (78" x 80")

Birds in Paradise has you coming and going! This quilt is completely reversible. The hand dyed cotton sateen fabrics, hand appliquéd by Cheri on the black sateen background, are absolutely stunning. I used very bright neon threads for all the quilting on the background and on the appliquéd motifs. The brightly colored thread made eye candy on the back of the beautiful hand dyed royal blue backing fabric. Cheri added roughly 900 Swarovski crystals on the front of this quilt and over 6100 on the back.

~ *Linda V. Taylor with Cheri Meineke-Johnson (hand appliqué and design)*

BIRDS IN PARADISE - BACK (78" x 80")

AWARDS:
Dallas Quilt Celebration: Best of Show, 2004
MQS: Best of Show, 2004
QTW: 1st Place, 2004
International Quilt Festival: Finalist, 2004
AQS: Gammill Quilting Award, 2005
Quilt Plano: Best of Show, 2005

Linda and Cheri were the pioneers of incorporating crystals into competition quilts. This quilt was displayed without a drape so the viewer could see both sides of the quilt as they passed it. This was the first quilt I had seen that had crystals added to the front and back. The quilting world has followed Linda and Cheri's lead. Today, many quilts display crystals interspersed with their quilting.

BEGINNING FEATHERS
THE SIMPLE FEATHER WREATH

Quilting for Show was originally a self-published How-To book. My goal was to teach machine quilters how to look like a hand quilter when using a domestic or longarm quilting machine. Even though this edition is completely different (revised and expanded), I wanted to include the step-by-step directions for achieving hand quilted effects. The following chapters are for those who like to see diagrams of the quilting path. The enclosed DVD provides additional visuals to learn how the motifs are quilted continuously. When I can see how something is done I can achieve it much easier. Any new technique will take some practice so don't give up after the first try. Keep at it until you can do it in your sleep!

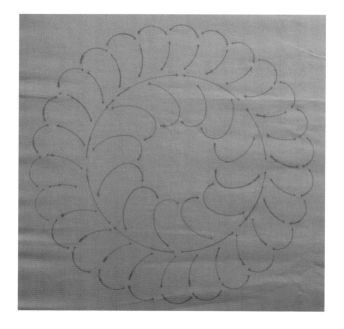

Nothing else is like a quilted, stenciled feather. It is formal, elegant and in control. Repeating this feather wreath throughout a quilt shows respect for traditional quilting. The feather wreath is a tried and true classic—a crowd pleaser for the last 100 years. From hand quilting to machine quilting, it works well every time. This chapter illustrates the quilting path you will need to follow to achieve the more formal look of a hand-quilted feather—by machine. Following the diagram will reduce thread build up, allow you to quilt continuously and enable you to achieve amazing results. Judges will notice your efforts and applaud you with comments such as, "Good backtracking."

Center your stencil and mark the stencil directly onto the fabric with a water or air soluble marker, or with a chalk pencil. You will start machine quilting in a spot that will hide your starting point. Quilt one feather then move into the center stem. Quilt the circle that makes up the center stem. For control, you can use any template or ruler to guide you as you are quilting. The illustration shows quilting clockwise, but if it's easier for you to quilt counter-clockwise then do that. Now you are ready to continue.

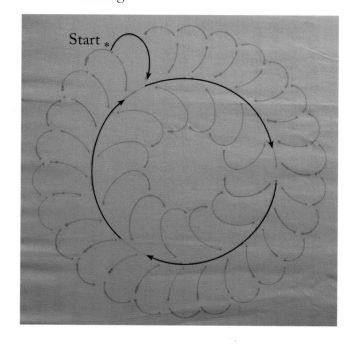

Start

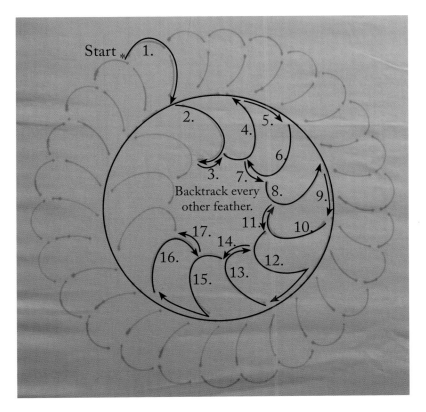

Start 1.

2.   5.
    4.
       6.
3.   7.
Backtrack every   8.
other feather.   9.
      11.   10.
17.   14.
16.   12.
15.   13.

*F*ollow the diagram arrows as shown. As you practice this technique you will master the path of the "every other one" method. A song could accompany this technique by singing, "Bump, Bump, Back, Over" and repeat. Stitch the inner feathers first, then backtrack out of the inner circle to get to the wreath's outer feathers. It's a good idea to complete any background quilting you want to do inside the wreath before you backtrack to the outer feathers.

*B*acktracking on every other feather as shown, will give your feather that hand-quilted look. Always backtrack over the feather humps, and never double stitch along the sides of the feather. More accurate backtracking can be achieved when using thin thread such as a 50 or 60 weight thread.

KAREN'S TIPS:

*I*f you are stippling your background you have another option for getting over the feather hump. Instead of backtracking, you could stipple over to the next feather. (Not shown.)

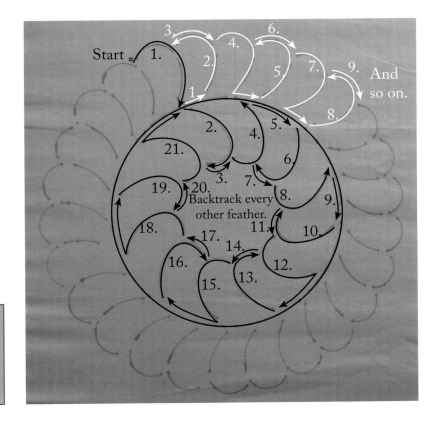

3.   6.
4.   9. And
Start 1.   2.   5.   7.   so on.
1.   8.
2.   5.
21.   4.   6.
    3.   7.
19.   20.   8.
Backtrack every   9.
other feather.
18.   11.   10.
17.   14.
16.   12.
15.   13.

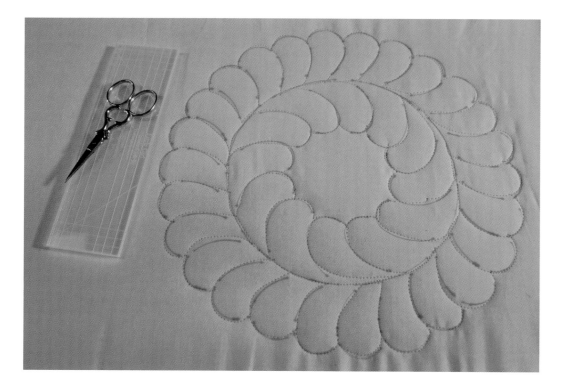

*U*sing a ruler to help guide you will add control while quilting the feather. When you are finished you can remove the markings and see the results.

*R*emoving the water soluable pen markings with an eraser pen will allow you to see your work right away—instant gratification. You can see how my feather looks like a traditional, hand quilted feather wreath but I did it all by machine.

INTERMEDIATE FEATHERS
ELEMENTAL QUILTING PATTERN

*H*ere is an example of a simple but elegant quilting design taken from my book, *The Secrets of Elemental Quilting*. It can be taken straight out of the book as shown here, or enlarged or reduced to fit. This design looks like a hand quilting design but there is a method to quilting it continuously, with minimal stopping and re-starting, by machine. Before you start, make sure your fabric is washed. You will be submerging this piece after quilting and you don't want your fabric colors to run.

*P*lace the design under the fabric and trace it with a water soluble pen or chalk pencil. Use a light box (found at most craft or sewing stores) if necessary. Don't let the fabric move. It's helpful to have an extra set of hands to help hold the fabric. Taping down the fabric helps keep it in place too.

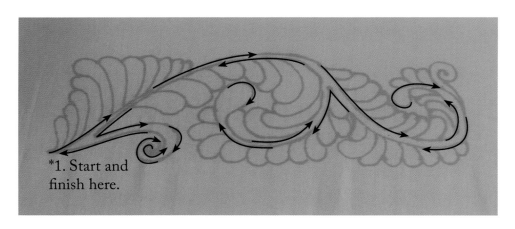

*1. Start and finish here.

The first step when you are quilting feathers is to quilt the stem. The arrows show you how to quilt the stem continuously, starting and stopping in the same place. The first feathers you quilt will also start in this spot. Use a ruler for greater control and to ensure that your stem lines are perfectly straight and ¼ inch a part.

The feathers are quilted using minimal backtracking, as shown. I call it the "bump, bump, back, over" method where you backtrack on every other feather to produce hand quilted effects.

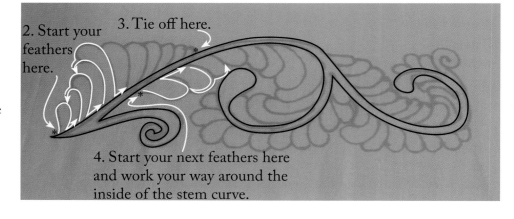

2. Start your feathers here.

3. Tie off here.

4. Start your next feathers here and work your way around the inside of the stem curve.

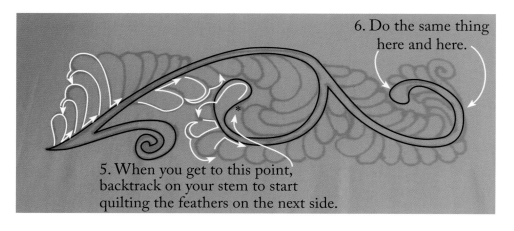

6. Do the same thing here and here.

5. When you get to this point, backtrack on your stem to start quilting the feathers on the next side.

Continue quilting, stopping to tie off (stop and restart) only if you have to. Backtrack whenever possible to reach the next spot you want to quilt.

*W*hen the design is completely quilted the markings can be removed by submerging the quilt in water.

*C*ongratulations, you have quilted an heirloom quilting design—which looks like a hand quilting pattern—by machine!

KAREN'S TIPS:

*U*sing a slightly darker thread helps bring out any motif that does not have trapunto. This is an old hand quilting trick to make your motif stand out a little more. The darker the thread, however, the more noticeable your starts and stops will be and it is recommended to bury your threads. Backtracking perfectly is harder using contrasting threads because if you miss the backtrack it will be very noticeable. Consider taking out the mistake and re-doing the feather.

There's a First Time for Everything (33" x 33")

I started making quilts about two years ago. I started to machine quilt with a mid-arm machine on a stand up frame about one year ago. I learned about wholecloth quilts from Karen's books. When I saw the designs in her book, *The Secrets of Elemental Quilting*, I knew I had to try to make one. I followed her instructions and drew some of her designs on a piece of muslin. I quilted it with my mid-arm machine. It came out better than I could have expected. I decided it needed a decorative binding edge. Now I had to learn to make a bias binding. Since this was the first time I ever attempted a wholecloth, a bias binding and decorative edge, the title seemed to fit. This was the first time I entered a show and the first time I won a ribbon. Now, I want to make more wholecloth quilts. The judges' comments were, "Stunning design with strong visual impact," "Excellent use of Trapunto" and "Excellent binding." I will be entering this in some national shows in the future.

~ *Carie Shields*

AWARDS: Columbia County Fair 2006:
Best of Show, Best Professional, Best Wallhanging and
1st Place Professional/ Wallhanging
Innovations: 1st Place Ribbon, Wholecloth, 2006

Carie took a class from me in Corvallis, Oregon where she casually mentioned during class that she had a wholecloth she wanted me to see which used designs from my book, *The Secrets of Elemental Quilting*. Even though it was her first wholecloth, she took the plunge and entered it in her local county fair. It took all the big ribbons at the county fair and blew away the other quilts. Not bad for a quilter with only a year of machine quilting experience who has never before entered a quilting competition. This is a great story for any quilter who feels reluctant to show her quilts or feels like a newbie. Carie felt all of those insecurities too, but did it anyway. She explained that there isn't any experience in her life that she can relate this to. She felt total shock and elation.

ADVANCED FEATHERS
FREEHAND FEATHERS

*Q*uilting feathers "freehand" is an advanced quilting technique. Freehand means the fabric isn't marked like when using a stencil. You will not know how your feather will look until the entire feather is quilted and finished. You will just need to trust that the feather will come out well. Using a thin thread helps hide your backtracking for this motif. Practice drawing freehand feathers on paper a few times if you need reassurance before starting your quilting. If you can master doing your feathers freehand, it shows your talent and passion. Freehand feathers are original and unique which is always helpful in competition. Judges know the difference between freehand and commercial stencils. You want a judge to think, "Wow, I have never seen that before!"

I like to use a ruler to control my stitches. I start by stitching in the ditch around the block. This stabilizes the block for the feather I'm going to quilt and it gives me a guideline to follow to shape the freehand feather.

*T*o begin, quilt the stem of the feather, giving it a little curve, and end in a pearl. Tie off and prepare to start quilting your feathers at the beginning of the stem. Since the feathers are not individually marked out, starting at the beginning is essential in order to bring the feathers into a nice form.

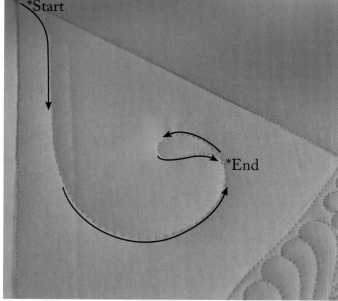

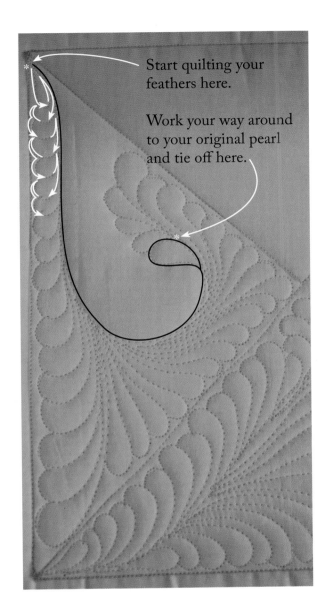

Start quilting your feathers here.

Work your way around to your original pearl and tie off here.

Start your feather at the beginning of your stem and quilt one side of the feather, working your way up to the pearl, using the "bump, bump, back, over" method. Stretch each feather as close to the ditch quilting as possible. This technique fills the entire space with quilting, enabling the quilter to avoid tight stippling or another background filler. When you reach your pearl, tie off and prepare to start quilting the inner feathers, starting from the beginning of your stem again.

Continue quilting along the stem, filling the empty space fully with feathers. Allow yourself to quilt irregular feathers—stretching them out, or elongating them. This is freehand after all. Finish the feather plume and tie off at the pearl.

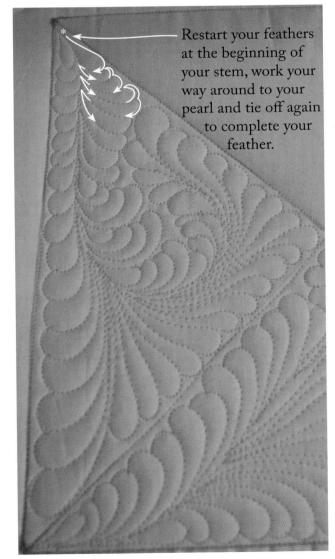

Restart your feathers at the beginning of your stem, work your way around to your pearl and tie off again to complete your feather.

KAREN'S TIPS:

Tying off at your pearl and restarting at your stem allows you to always feel like you are quilting in the correct or natural direction. For example, if I quilted from my pearl end towards my stem end (instead of from my stem end towards my pearl end) I would feel like I was quilting backwards— like trying to write my name from right to left instead of from left to right. It feels unnatural and it doesn't look as good.

A VISIT TO PROVENCE
(23½" x 23½")

*A*fter researching vintage Provence quilts, I made a list of design elements in many of them that would lend themselves to a miniature design, and then mapped out this wholecloth quilt on paper. The central formal arrangement was drawn and then traced onto the quilt top, as were the lines for the wreath circle and the outer border vines, but the feathers were quilted freehand. The feather groups in the border were also quilted freehand with no drawing, so they all are a bit different. The quilting fills the spaces created by the vine undulations, much like the actual Provence quilts. Typical fan quilting motifs complete the four corners of the inner square, and the tiny circles, like a string of pearls, in the feathered vine and wreath are true to those done in actual hand quilted full size Provencal quilts.

I was so delighted with my new sewing machine that I wanted to really stretch my skills with it and see if I could make something in miniature to show what a marvelous tool it was. I knew right away that to try and mark designs this small was futile, but if I could give myself some marked guidelines it might work. I did use the magnifier on my machine for the very fine feathers and backgrounds. Quilting traditional formal designs like this but doing it freehand opened my mind to the possibilities of doing it all the time, and since this quilt I have been working frequently with no lines, without that safety net, and loving it. When I finished this quilt I knew I had graduated to a new level of skill combined with artistry. I don't think I could replicate this quilt; the planets were all aligned for that 2-week period I worked on it. I think the quilt forged new ground for quality in machine quilting and showed what a determined quilter could do on a home sewing machine. Judges' Comments: "Perfection in machine quilting." ~ *Diane Gaudynski*

AWARDS:

AQS:
First Place Miniatures, 2004
NQA:
First Place Miniatures, 2004
QOTW:
S. Schamber's Faculty Ribbon, 2004
IQA:
Second Place Miniatures, 2005

*D*iane quilted her feathers freehand. Freehand, I tell you. This means little marking of the quilt top. In general we define this technique as pure, crazy, wondrous talent. Diane can produce quilts that are inspired by history and respect the quilting tradition, but still push the envelope by using machine quilting and by quilting with miniscule stitches. She does it with style and grace. Her ground-breaking quilting has ensured that the days of judges counting 10 to 12 stitches per inch are over. Today's stitch regulated machines allow you to stitch as small as you dare. Consistency in stitch length will result in judges who are pleased with the overall impact of the quilt.

QUILTING ROPE & CABLE

This chapter reviews a few stencils on the market that are generally sold to hand-quilters. Starting with a simple rope border and progressing all the way to a cable and feather combo border, the diagrams will walk you through the path for any machine quilting. The result will make your quilt stand out and shine above the competition.

SIMPLE ROPE BORDER

You can use this stencil as a border or in sashing. I think it is most effective on country style quilting. If the rope is continued throughout the sashing or small borders, it gives the quilt a well planned look. Judges find this appealing. I have many different rope stencils in all different sizes to accommodate different sized sashing. This rope stencil can be machine quilted with ease and still appear hand-quilted. Once you learn the technique of the "every other one" method, you will be able to apply the same technique to the rope.

Start by marking your stencil to fit.

Follow the arrows as shown. It's, "Bump, Bump, Back, Over." Do not backtrack in the centers of the rope. Only one stitching path should be present in the segments.

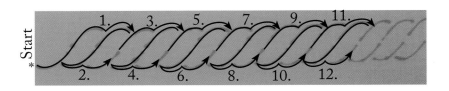

Here is the quilted border with the markings.

SIMPLE CABLE BORDER

Cables are also a motif which requires a little bit of skill to master quilting continuously. The cable is meant to look like it's full of stopping and starting, but you don't actually want to stop and start while you are quilting. The diagrams below will show you how to get through the entire motif without quilting through the intersections, which judges would call a short cut.

Mark your stencil design to fit.

Start where you see a beginning to a cable segment. We will not stop and re-start anywhere in the cable—it will all be continuous machine quilting. Follow the diagram as shown and use thin thread to hide your thread path.

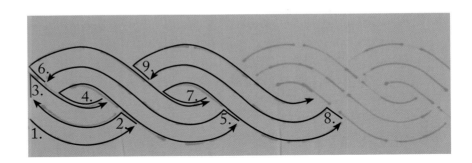

Using a ruler template will help you with control if you are using a longarm. Otherwise it's just a matter of following the markings.

CABLE AND FEATHER BORDER

The Cable and Feather stencil is an impressive stencil which has been around the quilting world for years and years. The Cable and Feather is somewhat advanced because it is challenging to make the connections look smooth and seamless. I generally mark my corners first with the Cable and Feather stencil, and then mark the center of the border. This makes joining the elements much easier because your eye will not see any modifications - such as stretching or shortening the design to fit.

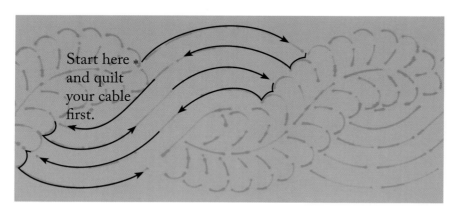

Mark your stencil design to fit. There is no stopping and starting with this diagram even though you will do one segment at a time. First quilt in the cable, then move on to finish the feather. There is lots of backtracking throughout this motif so do not get discouraged. You will notice that the backtracking gets easier as you continue to quilt the motif.

Quilt the feather's stem before quilting the feathers. Work your way from right to left on the lower side of the feather, backtracking on every other feather, then work way back from left to right on the upper side of the feather. This will bring you to your next starting point on the cable.

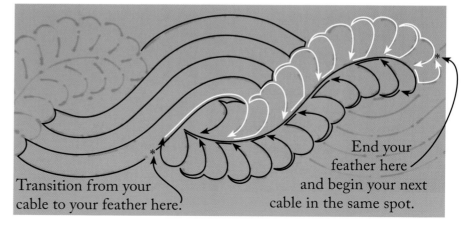

Here is the result of the quilting with the markings. The more precise you are in your backtracking, the more your motif will look handquilted.

CUSTOM ROPE WREATH

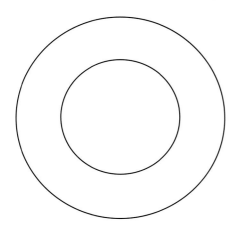

*T*he Rope Wreath is perfect for large plain blocks. It is easy to create your very own custom rope wreath to fit a specific size or unusual space. To start, you will need something to help you mark a circle and one rope border stencil. Mark two circles approximately 1- 2 inches apart from each other as shown.

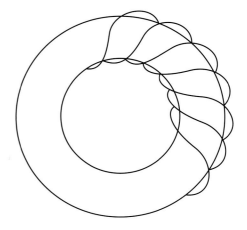

*P*lace the stencil at an angle directly over the circles. Look through the stencil to find your placement. Mark 1 segment then rotate the stencil slightly so your rope will line up on the circle for the next segment.

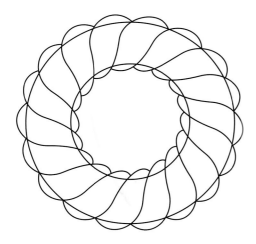

*C*ontinue marking your segments until you are completely around the circle. You have to "nudge" in the last segment to fit in the circle. (See tip.)

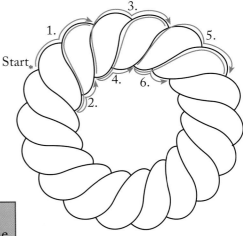

*S*titch the rope stencil using the same techniques as the feather ("bump, bump, back, over" or "every other one" technique). Tie off at your starting point or continue to quilt your background grid/design.

KAREN'S TIPS:

*I*f you mark in the circle using even numbers (such as a 10 inch, 12 inch or 14 inch circle) the segments or rope sections will blend together without much "nudging."

STRAIGHT LINE QUILTING

Background quilting fillers highlight the motifs and in terms of construction, keep the quilt layers together. It's important to use proper quilting background elements and to know when and where to place them. I like to add as many difficult background filler designs as possible in a quilt, and show some freehand filler work as well, without combining too many different odd angles of straight line quilting, which would be distracting. I try to balance each of the background fillers throughout the body of the quilt so they look good next to each other. I don't recommend using freehand background fillers on an entire quilt. This shows a judge that you do not want to attempt anything difficult, like straight line quilting. Straight line quilting, such as crosshatching, is difficult because you will need accuracy. If your quilted line is wobbly, points are taken away on the score card.

CHEVRON

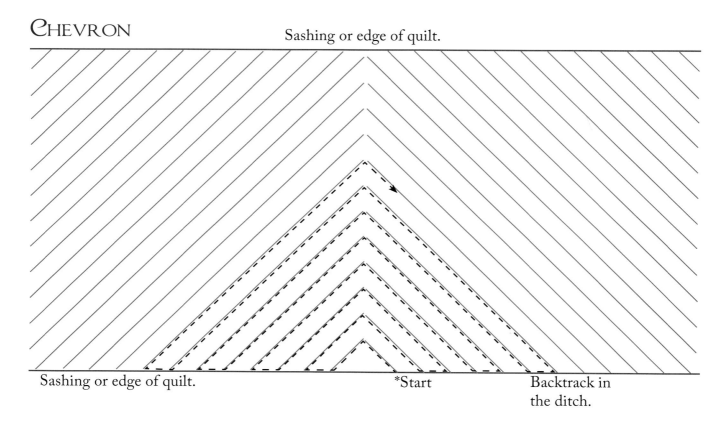

Sashing or edge of quilt.

Sashing or edge of quilt.

*Start

Backtrack in the ditch.

This design will bring your eye directly to the middle of the chevron. It is very traditional to use this filler in a larger space, such as a border. To start, mark your chevron directly on the fabric using a water soluble pen or a chalk pencil. You can use a plastic commercial stencil or a ruler, following the 45 degree angle. When you are quilting straight lines, it's really nice to have a stitch regulator. Your stitches will look a lot better if they are perfectly consistent. Try to continuously quilt this design, without stopping and starting by starting in the center, as shown, and backtracking along the ditch to get to the next line in the chevron.

DIAGONAL LINES

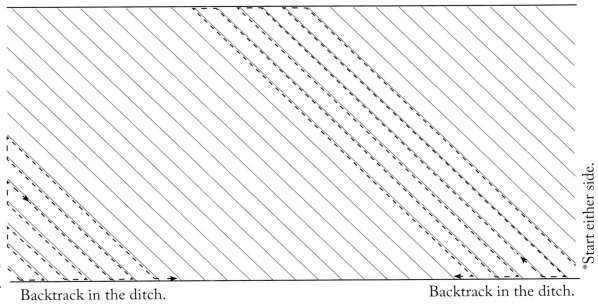

This design is easy to draw on fabric, as well as to quilt. Draw out your diagonal lines, angled at 45 degrees, using a commercial stencil or a ruler, choosing ¼ inch, ½ inch or 1 inch spaces between your lines. Follow the arrows as shown to quilt this background filler continuously.

DOUBLE DIAGONAL/ PIANO KEYS

This technique is a little more decorative than plain diagonal lines but the quilting pattern is just the same. Draw out your diagonal lines, angled at 45 degrees, using a commercial stencil or a ruler, alternating between thick and thin spaces. For example, draw your lines with a ¼ inch of space and then a ½ inch of space, or ½ inch and then 1 inch, etc. Follow the arrows as shown to quilt this background filler continuously.

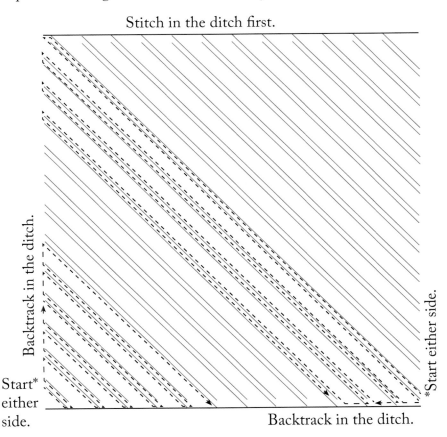

CROSSHATCHING

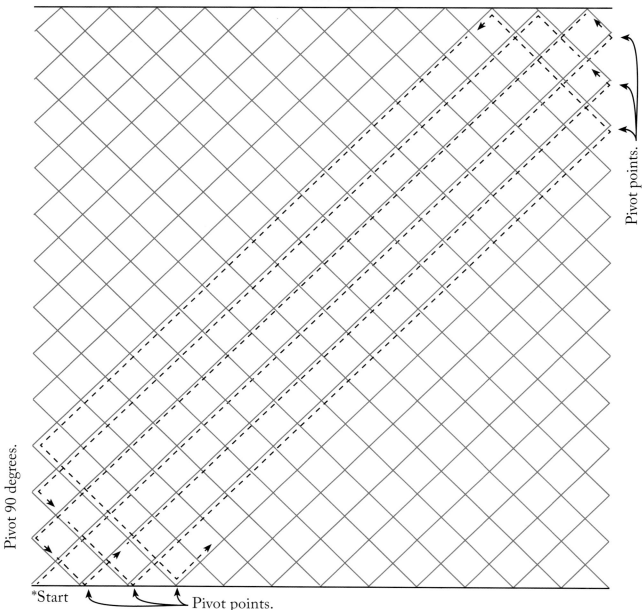

Stitch in the ditch first.

Pivot points.

Pivot 90 degrees.

*Start   Pivot points.

Crosshatching continuously is a challenge. It is time consuming but we want to get through it quickly and accurately. This diagram will show you how to get through the area without re-starting after each line. I always use a commercial stencil for marking my crosshatching. They come in many sizes but my favorite is the ½ inch crosshatching stencil. Lay your stencil down on your fabric and start marking; always move the stencil from left to right as you mark. Never mark clockwise or counter clockwise—you won't be able to line up the lines perfectly in the end. When you are done marking you can start your stitching anywhere you would like. When you reach the point where the crosshatching ends and you see a "V," pivot 90 degrees making another side of a square. Keep making this box, over and over again and you will make it through the entire piece without having to stop and re-start.

ORANGE PEEL OR WINE GLASS

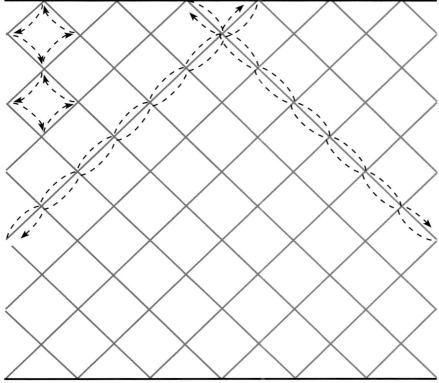

Stitch in the ditch first.

If you want a more complicated quilting design, you can quilt what is called "Orange Peel" or "Wine Glass" after you have marked your crosshatching grid (for the smallest orange peel, I like to use a ½ inch crosshatching stencil). To start, mark your crosshatching grid on the fabric. Then quilt a small curve along each segment as shown. There are a couple of options shown and I'm sure there are other ways to quilt this pattern too. Develop your own pattern and rhythm to your curves as you quilt so the direction is easy for you to remember and you won't forget any spaces. After the entire grid is quilted, remove your markings, and the continuous curve will look very controlled and accurate.

KAREN'S TIPS:

To achieve ¼ inch crosshatching, quilt between your already quilted ½ inch crosshatching lines. Follow your lines perfectly using your hopping foot as a guide or use a ruler to guide your foot at a 45 degree angle. Repeat the same process of making a "box" and you will get through ¼ inch crosshatching (continuously) as well.

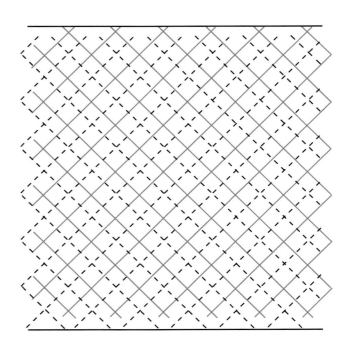

BECAUSE IT'S JUST HARDER TO APPLIQUÉ (89" x 94")

AWARDS:

Minnesota State Fair: 1st Place, Wholecloth, 2003
Minnesota State Fair: Best in Show, Longarm, 2003
Minnesota State Fair: Sweepstakes Award, 2003
Minnesota Quilters Show and Conference: Best of Show Longarm, 2003

This original, wholecloth quilt is the result of learning from mistakes I have made on prior wholecloth quilts. This wholecloth combines color trapunto with traditional trapunto. The color comes from bright red acrylic felt used under the quilt top fabric as trapunto batting, which creates a shadow of pink. I used several different red and pink felts to achieve the different hues in the trapunto. I developed a cut-away trapunto technique after trying many different types of fibers and methods for trapunto. The cut-away method using acrylic felt seemed to be the most successful. The backing is cotton sateen. This is the most rewarding wholecloth I have ever designed and quilted because disaster was avoided. ~ *Karen McTavish*

KAREN'S FINAL THOUGHTS

I self-published the first edition of *Quilting for Show*. It was nothing more than a flip book that you could lay on your quilt as you quilted. It was basic hand drawings and chicken scratches in a calendar style book. My vision for re-publishing this book was to take the mystery out of quilting competition, but more importantly, to take the fear out of it. Fear is what sets anyone back from taking big powerful steps in life. My goal for the reader of the new *Quilting for Show* is for you to listen to that little voice that says, "I could do that," and

go with it. No matter what your insecurities say, do it anyway and ignore the fear. One magnificent quilt in your lifetime will NOT kill you. Take your time, do the hardest thing, never take a short cut and your quilt will do very well in show. What is the real secret to winning quilting awards? Being fearless when you are scared out of your mind.

Best of Show wishes!

KAREN'S BIO

*L*ongarm machine quilting allows Karen to combine her two passions: Wholecloth and Trapunto. Karen specializes in crafting award-winning quilts using techniques which allow machine quilters to replicate traditional "hand quilted" effects. She has been featured on PBS's *Quilt Central* and HGTV's *Simply Quilts*. Her work has appeared in Joanne Line's books, *Quilts from the Quilt Makers Gift #1* and *#2*, and numerous national magazines and journals. Karen's other books, *Mastering the Art of McTavishing* and *The Secrets of Elemental Quilting* are available through her website. Karen has been a full-time professional longarm quilter since 1997—supporting herself and her family through her craft. Karen lives on Lake Superior's North Shore, quilting and teaching from her studio and throughout the country. She has two children, Ally and Storm.

Contact her at:
Karen McTavish
728 N 18th Ave East
Duluth, MN 55812
Phone: (218) 391-8218
Fax: (218) 525-0017
or visit her website at
www.designerquilts.com

CONTRIBUTING QUILTERS

Kim Brunner
19826 Burlington Path
Farmington, MN 55024
Phone: 651-463-6705
Email: Kimmyquilt@aol.com

Hollis Chatelain
909 Lawrence Road
Hillsborough, NC 27278
Phone: 919-732-5119
Email: hollis@hollisart.com
Website: www.hollisart.com

Caryl Bryer Fallert
Bryerpatch Studio
502 North 5th St.
Paducah, KY 42001
Phone: 270-444-8040
Email: caryl@bryerpatch.com
Website: www.bryerpatch.com

Myrna Ficken
2332 West Ridge View Drive
Hurricane UT 84737
Phone: 435-635-7900
Cell: 435-229-2703
Email: myrna@tksinc.us
Website: www.aquilterschoice.com

Diane Gaudynski
PO Box 448
Pewaukee, WI 53072
Email: diane@dianegaudynski.net
Website: www.dianegaudynski.net

Anita Kris Mattson
1219 Colonization Rd. W.
Fort Frances, Ontario
P9A 2T6 Canada
Phone: 807-274-7218
Email: lmatty@shaw.ca

Linda McCuean
301 Sylvania Drive
New Galilee, PA 16141
Phone: 724-336-6513
Cell: 724-622-0136
Email: lindamccuean@yahoo.com

Sharon Schamber
1304 W. Stirrup Way
Payson, AZ 85541
Phone: 928-474-9143
Cell: 801-718-5048
Email: schamber@npgcable.com
Website: www.sharonschamber.com

Carol A. Selepec
Create A Stitch
17 7th Street
Midland, PA 15059
Studio Phone: 724-643-4833
Email: createastitch@verizon.net

Carie Shields
Sew Now What?
St. Helens, OR
Cell: 503-201-5323
Email: cshields62@yahoo.com

Linda V. Taylor
4964 US Hwy 75 North
Melissa, TX 75454
Phone: 972-542-4000
Cell: 972-529-7459
Email: linda@lequilters.com
Website: www.lequilters.com

Ricky Tims c/o
Tims Art Quilt Studio and Gallery
105 W. Ryus Ave./PO Box 392
La Veta, CO 81055
Phone: 719-742-3795
Email: info@rickytims.com
Website: www.rickytims.com

PRODUCTS & PEOPLE MENTIONED IN THE BOOK

APQS
American Professional Quilting Systems
8033 University Ave. Suite F
Des Moines IA 50325
Phone: 800-426-7233
Fax: 515-267-8414
Email: sales@apqs.com
Website: www.apqs.com

*Karen McTavish is an APQS representative.
Please contact Karen directly for any questions
regarding an APQS longarm quilting machine.
Phone: 218-391-8218
Email: kmctavish@designerquilts.com
Website: www.designerquilts.com

Superior Threads
87 East 2580 South
St. George, UT 84790
Phone: 435-652-1867
Toll free: 800-499-1777
Email: info@superiorthreads.com
Website: www.superiorthreads.com

The Gadget Girls
Gadget Girl Rulers and Templates
12907 Oak Plaza Drive
Cypress, TX 77429
Phone: 281-890-4222
Toll Free: 888-844-8537
Fax: 281-890-9276
Email: shelly@thegadgetgirls.com
Website: www.thegadgetgirls.com

Cheri Meineke-Johnson
Cheri's Crystals
Phone: 940-497-6399
Website: www.cheriscrystals.com

Pat Harrison - Ocean Waves Quilting Company
Longarm Quilting, Longarm Lessons, Guild Lectures
59 Reuben Brown Lane / Exeter, RI 02822
Phone: 401-667-0214
Email: oceanwavesqc@cox.net
Website: http://community.webshots.com/user/owqc1

Pepper Cory
Quilting Judge, Author and Quiltmaker
203 First Street
Beaufort, North Carolina 28516
Email: pepcory@mail.clis.com
Website: www.peppercory.com

Jean Carlton
AQS Quilt Appraiser
Maple Grove, MN
Phone: 952-240-9187
Email: quiltsetc@comcast.net

Helen Squire
Technical Advisor for the American Quilter's
Society's television show, American Quilter,
Author, Instructor, Designer and Vice-President of
Sales & Marketing for AQS.
American Quilter's Society
PO Box 3290
Paducah, KY 42002-3290
Phone: 270-898-7903
Fax: 270-898-1173
Email: helen@AQSquilt.com
Website: www.AQSquilt.com

QUILT SHOWS DEFINED

American Quilter's Society (AQS): www.americanquilter.com

Columbia County Fair: www.columbiafair.com/competition.html

Dakota County Fair: www.dakotacountyfair.org

Dallas Quilt Celebration: www.quiltersguildofdallas.org

Innovations: www.mqinnovations.com

International Quilt Association (IQA): www.quilts.org

International Quilt Festival: www.quilts.com

Las Vegas Guild Quilt Show: (no website)

Lowell Quilt Festival (LQF): www.lowellquiltfestival.org

Machine Quilter's Exposition (MQX): www.mqxshow.com

Machine Quilter's Showcase (MQS): www.imqa.org

Mid-Atlantic Quilt Festival: www.quiltfest.com

Mid-Valley Quilt Guild Show: (no website)

Minnesota Quilters State Quilt Show: www.mnquilt.org

National Quilting Association Show (NQA): www.nqaquilts.org

Pacific International Quilt Festival: www.quiltfest.com

Pennsylvania National Quilt Extravaganza: www.quiltfest.com

Quilter's Heritage Celebration (QHC): www.qhconline.com/artman/publish/

Quilting on the Waterfront (QTQ/QTW/QOTW): www.quiltingonthewaterfront.com

Quilting by the Lake: www.quiltingbythelake.com

Quilt Odyssey: www.quiltodyssey.com

Quilt Plano: www.quiltersguildofplano.org

Quintessential Quilt St. Louis: www.qquilters.org

Road to California: www.road2ca.com

Rockome Gardens, Rockome, IL: (no website)

Thirty Distinguished Quiltmakers in the World, Tokyo, Japan: (no website)

, many other shows around the country and around the world. To find more cal guild, look in quilting magazines or search the internet.

DVD TABLE OF CONTENTS

Problems with your DVD?

First, try playing your DVD on another DVD player or on your computer. Also, if you are playing your DVD on your computer, make sure you have a DVD drive, not just a CD drive. DVD's and CD's look the same but they are not. If you are having trouble getting the whole DVD to play in sequence on your DVD player, go back to the "main menu" on your DVD and highlight each chapter that you want to view. Not all DVD players will play the DVD from start to finish.

This DVD is designed to play from start to finish or in parts. To play a specific section, select the desired lesson from the main menu. This DVD has been formatted to play on NTSC machines in North America. NTSC formatting should work in newer DVD's and TV's from Europe, Australia, New Zealand and Asia as well. If you are from a country which supports PAL formatting, and you can't get the DVD to play, or it plays in black and white, try playing the DVD in your computer or on a newer DVD player with an NTSC compatible TV.

Write to us at contactus@onwordboundbooks.com and let us know if you are having a problem playing your DVD. We will work to resolve the problem and if your DVD is cracked or defective, we will replace it.